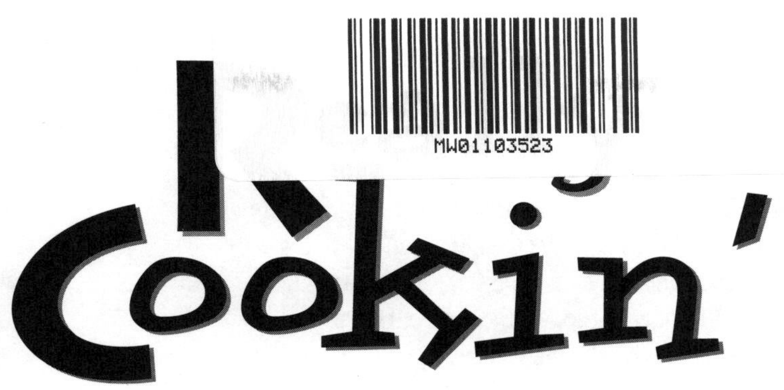

By Carol Ferguson

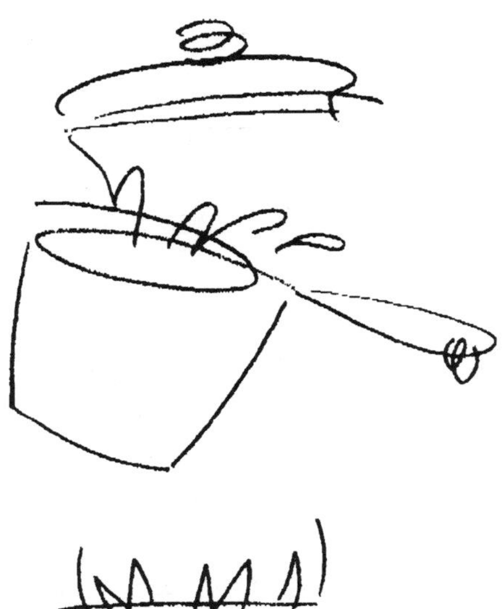

Maxwell Macmillan Canada

Maxwell Macmillan Canada
1200 Eglinton Avenue East, Suite 200
Don Mills, Ontario
M3C 3N1

Canadian Cataloguing in Publication Data

Ferguson, Carol
Really cookin'

ISBN 0-02-954174-3

1. Cookery. I. Title.

TX714.F47 1994 641.5'12 C94-931298-3

Design: Heidy Lawrance Associates

Cover design: Wycliffe Smith Design Inc.

Illustration: Kathryn Adams: Three In a Box

Production Co-ordinator: Stephanie Cox

Back cover photograph of Carol Ferguson by Birgitte Nielsen. With thanks to The Green Garden, Bloor Street West, Toronto, and to Kevin Auguste, Jeanie Paolella, Christopher Rizzo, Alenka Skara.

Printed and bound in Canada

94 95 96 97 98 5 4 3 2 1

CONTENTS

INTRODUCTION

Good food is one of the great pleasures of life, and cooking can be half the fun. Good cooking doesn't have to be complicated or expensive. Some of the best food in the world comes from the simplest ingredients simply prepared.

Good food is *real* food. It looks good and tastes wonderful. It's full of natural flavours and textures and colours. It makes you feel good. It nourishes your body and soul and keeps you healthy and happy.

Do you want great food that's easy to make? Are you a student? A beginning cook? Someone who is living away from home for the first time and wants to bail out of a steady diet of packaged macaroni and take-out pizza? Or are you simply short of time and know-how? This book will teach you basic cooking skills and provide you with lots of inspiration.

With over 100 no-fail recipes using easy-to-find ingredients and easy-to-follow instructions, plus lots of menu suggestions, there's something for every day and every special occasion.

You'll find easy versions of your favourite fast foods, traditional comfort food, great party food, healthy snacks and popular international cooking.

Whether it's a family dinner with all your favourite dishes, a celebration feast with friends or just a nice solitary supper at the end of a long day, some of your most satisfying meals can come from your own good cooking. I hope this book gets you off to a good start. Read, cook, eat and enjoy!

Carol Ferguson

HOW TO USE THIS BOOK

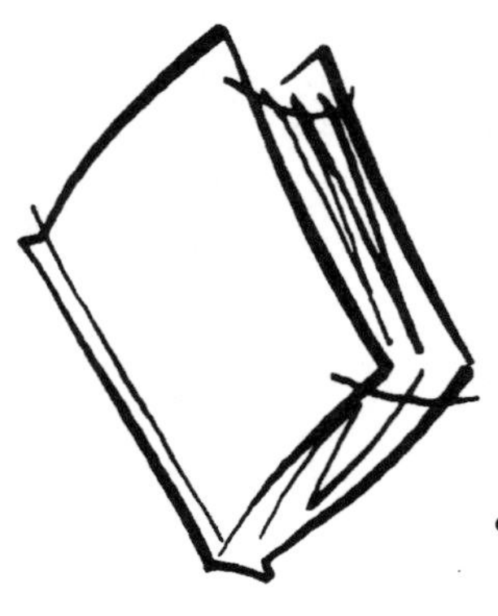

- Start with the easiest recipes (try Taco Dip, Greek Salad, Baked Potatoes with Toppings or Wacky Cake). Move on to some simple meat and vegetable dishes (Easy Oven Stew, Stir-fried Chicken & Vegetables). Try your hand at some baking (Banana Bread, Quick Cinnamon Rolls). Make a simple supper for yourself and a friend (maybe Pasta Primavera or Barbecued Spareribs with a salad). Soon you'll be putting together three-course menus (see suggestions on page 102). Throw a party! Invite your friends! Impress your mom! You might even get asked for your recipe. Now you're *Really Cookin'*!
- If you're a student in a foods or nutrition course, this book can be used in both classroom and home kitchens. If you're cooking at school, your teacher might use the recipes as a series of cooking lessons or to illustrate basic techniques, meal planning, food shopping, nutrition or applied food chemistry. If your course doesn't include classroom cooking, try the recipes at home to add hands-on experience in the kitchen, to learn the practical skills, and to enjoy the pleasures of cooking.
- The recipes in this book are simple to make without using a lot of packages and mixes. You learn to cook by *really cooking.* As you work through the recipes, you'll learn basic cooking techniques, how to measure, how to handle basic ingredients—and how *real* food is supposed to taste.
- When trying a new recipe:
  1. Read the recipe through to make sure you have all the ingredients and equipment, and that you understand each step in the method (for unfamiliar terms and techniques, see page 8).
  2. If the ingredients are listed as partially prepared (eg chopped, sliced), do this before you start the steps in the method.
  3. Assemble the ingredients so you can reach them easily as you work.

4. Follow the recipe steps in order.

- If you're on your own and need help with the recipes, consult a family member or friend who knows his or her way around the kitchen.
- Cooking for company: choose a menu of recipes you've made before and are comfortable with; do as much ahead as possible so you can relax.
- Cook with your friends and learn together. Cooking and eating are the most fun as a shared activity.
- Microwave cooking: If you have a microwave oven, use the owner's manual for basic instructions and recipes. Be careful to use dishes recommended for microwaves. There are also lots of microwave cookbooks in libraries and bookstores.
- Using the proper equipment makes cooking much easier but until you collect all the gear, make do with what you have; use a bottle instead of a rolling pin, a glass for a cookie cutter, foil or a pieplate for a lid.
- Don't be afraid to adjust recipes to your taste or available ingredients. Follow the recipes carefully at first to learn basic techniques and to get a general guide to seasonings. Then, as you get more experience, taste and adjust as you go along—decide what *you* like. Make up your own variations and note them on the recipes.
- The only time you shouldn't adjust recipes is when baking. A cake or quickbread recipe is a carefully balanced formula (a good lesson in food chemistry); you'll get the same results every time if you measure accurately (see page 10).
- Start your own recipe collection in a notebook or binder. Collect favourites from family and friends and try out interesting recipes from magazines, newspapers and cookbooks.
- Expand your own tastes and food experiences. Canadian cooking includes lots of local and regional specialties as well a whole world of international flavours. Just check out the selection at any really good supermarket (there are probably hundreds of items you didn't know were

there). Explore farmers' markets, city markets in ethnic neighbourhoods, specialty food shops. Talk to the butcher the baker, the greengrocer; ask lots of questions and try something new. Browse in kitchen shops and cookbook stores. Sample all the goodies at multicultural food fairs. Accept any and all invitations to eat out in interesting restaurants (and especially at friends' homes with traditional cooking different from yours).

CANADA'S FOOD GUIDE TO HEALTHY EATING

Eating well means making good food choices. The Food Guide tells you the kinds of foods to choose and how much you need every day. (Copies are available from your local or provincial health department.)

- Choose a *variety* of foods from each of the 4 food groups each day: **Grain Products, Vegetables & Fruit, Milk Products, Meat & Alternatives.**
- Choose whole grain and enriched products more often.
- Choose dark green and orange vegetables and orange fruits more often.
- Choose lower-fat milk products more often.
- Choose leaner meats, poultry and fish, and dried peas, beans and lentils more often.
- Maintain a healthy body weight by being active and eating well.

EQUIPMENT FOR A BASIC KITCHEN

Learning to cook is much easier with good equipment, but you don't need a lot. If you're starting from scratch or have a limited space and budget, you can get by with only a few essentials at first. Start with a good knife, skillet and saucepan (the best you can beg, borrow or buy). Then gradually add the equipment you really need and want as you expand your cooking skills. This list will take you through all the recipes in this book:

KNIVES

A good knife is your most important tool. Cheap knives with dull blades are frustrating to use and more dangerous than sharp, high-quality knives. Good knives are expensive but will last a lifetime; the best are high-carbon stainless steel with the blade running the full length of the handle; they feel balanced and comfortable in your hand. Keep them sharpened and use only on a cutting board. To protect the blade from damage, store it in a wooden rack or on a magnetic holder, not in a drawer. Start with these three:

- **paring or utility knife** (5 to 7-inch/12 to 18 cm) for peeling and cutting
- **all-purpose chef's knife** (10-inch/25 cm with wide blade) for chopping and slicing
- **serrated bread knife** (10-inch/25 cm).

POTS AND PANS

- **Skillet/frying pan** (10-inch/25 cm) with lid; choose a pan of good weight with a non-stick surface.
- **Two saucepans** (4-cup/1L and 8-cup/2L) with lids. Heavy-bottomed pots are best, such as stainless steel with a thick bottom of layered metals for good heat distribution, or enamelled cast iron or aluminum with a non-stick surface. Lightweight pans don't cook evenly and cause food to stick and burn.

- **Large pot** (16-cup/4 L) with lid, for pasta and soup.
- **Broiler pan** (or metal baking pan with rack).

BOWLS AND BAKING DISHES

Many bowls and dishes are multi-purpose. Ovenproof glass and ceramic baking dishes can also be used in the microwave and as serving dishes. You'll likely also use your dinnerware (plates and small bowls) for food preparation. For baking, aluminum pans are best; they bake evenly and don't rust.

- **Three mixing bowls** (small, medium, large): stainless steel, glass or pottery
- **Three baking dishes/casseroles** (4-cup/1 L, 6-cup/1.5 L, 8-cup/2 L) preferably with lids
- **Glass custard cups** (2 or 3 for storage and microwave)
- **Glass pie plate** (9-inch/1 L)
- **Rectangular baking pan** (13 x 9 x 2-inch /3.5 L)
- **Square cake pans** (8-inch/2 L and 9-inch/2.5 L)
- **Loaf pan** (8 ½ x 4 ½-inch/1.5 L)
- **Muffin tins**
- **Shallow baking pan/jelly roll pan** (15 x 10 x ¾-inch/2L); can also be used as baking sheet
- **Baking sheet** without sides (best for cookies); optional
- **Serving bowls and platter**

TOOLS

- **Measuring cups and spoons** (see page 10)
- **Cutting board** (wood or plastic)
- **Long handled tools: mixing spoon, slotted spoon, wide spatula/lifter** (use nylon or plastic for non-stick pots and pans)
- **Rubber spatula**
- **Wire whisk**
- **Wooden spoon**
- **Pastry brush**
- **Sieve (wire mesh)**

- **Large colander**
- **Soup ladle**
- **Egg beater**
- **Grater**
- **Can opener**
- **Kitchen scissors**
- **Vegetable peeler**
- **Potato masher**
- **Pepper grinder**
- **Pastry blender**
- **Rolling pin**
- **Wire cooling rack**

SMALL APPLIANCES (optional)

- **Electric kettle**
- **Toaster or toaster oven**
- **Electric mixer** (makes baking much easier; handheld models are inexpensive)
- **Electric blender or food processor**
- **Microwave oven:** A compact model is fine. A microwave is the busy cook's best friend for saving time and energy in preparation, cooking and clean-up, thawing frozen food and heating leftovers.

Also make sure your **fridge** and **stove** are in good working order. Many old ovens don't have accurate temperature dials; check the temperature with a reliable oven thermometer. If the oven dial is off a few degrees, you can adjust it each time it's used; if it's off a lot (more than 25°C), it should be fixed.

TERMS & TECHNIQUES

Recipes use specific terms for different cooking and baking techniques. Here are some of the basics you should know:

Baste: Spoon or brush liquid (pan drippings or sauce) over food during cooking to keep it moist or add flavour.

Beat: Mix vigorously until smooth or to introduce air; easiest with electric mixer; also done with egg beater, wire whisk, spoon, or fork.

Chop: Cut in small pieces (fine, medium or coarse) with sharp knife; minced means very finely chopped; **diced** means tiny cubes.

Cream: Usually refers to mixing butter with sugar; beat with electric mixer or wooden spoon until thoroughly blended and light in texture.

Cut in: Usually refers to mixing fat into flour (for pastry or biscuits). Easiest with a wire pastry blender; cut through the fat until it is in tiny pieces and the mixture looks like coarse crumbs. (You could also use two knives, scissor-fashion, or just rub fat into flour with your fingertips.)

Fold: Usually refers to combining stiffly-beaten egg whites or whipped cream with another mixture; the purpose is to blend without losing any of the volume. Using a rubber spatula, move it down one side of the bowl, across the bottom and up the other side; turn bowl slightly and repeat, folding the mixture together gently (don't stir) until no white bits of egg or cream remain.

Grease: Brush baking pan lightly with fat to prevent sticking (shortening is best; butter tends to brown too much and oil doesn't coat well enough). To **grease and flour** a pan: Brush with fat, then sprinkle with flour; tap pan to distribute flour in a light, even coating; tap out any excess.

Knead: Usually refers to firm pressing and folding of yeast dough to make it smooth and springy, but gentle kneading is also used for quickbreads such as biscuits. Place ball of dough on floured surface; with fingertips, lift dough towards you, folding it in half; press down with the heels of the hands. Give dough a quarter turn and repeat (about 10 times for biscuits, up to 10 minutes for yeast bread).

Marinate: Cover food with a liquid mixture and set aside for a period of time to develop flavour or tenderize.

Mix or **Blend:** Combine ingredients until evenly distributed.

Sauté: Fry quickly in a little fat over high heat.

Simmer: Cook at just below boiling; liquid should be moving but not bubbling hard.

Stir: Mix thoroughly with a spoon without beating.

Stir-fry: In large pan with small amount of oil over high heat, use large spoon or spatula to stir and turn pieces of food quickly and constantly.

Testing for doneness (cakes, quick breads): Insert a large wooden toothpick, cocktail pick or thin skewer into centre; it should come out clean with no moist particles clinging to it.

Whisk: Mix briskly with a wire whisk.

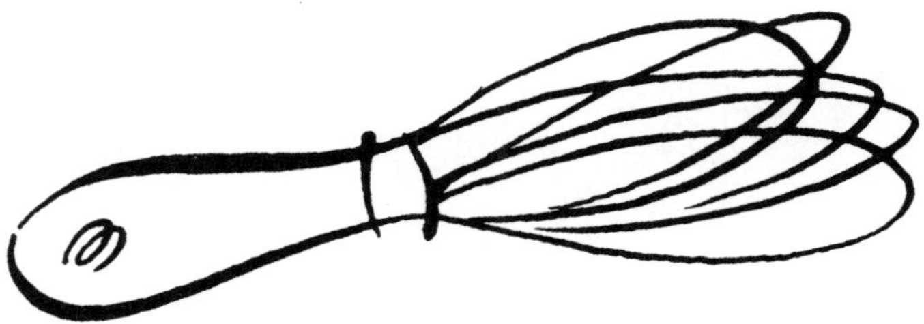

MEASURING

When using a recipe that gives dual measures (metric and imperial), it is important to use only one system or the other, not a combination of both as they are not exact equivalents. (In this book, imperial is on the left of the ingredient lists, metric on the right.)

Be sure to buy standard measuring sets, either metric or imperial:

Metric:
Three dry measures (250 mL, 125 mL, 50 mL)
Five small measures (25 mL, 15 mL, 5 mL, 2 mL, 1 mL)

Imperial:
Four measuring cups (1 cup, ½ cup, ⅓ cup, ¼ cup)
Four measuring spoons (1 tbsp,1 tsp, ½ tsp, ¼ tsp)

To measure dry ingredients, spoon into cup and level off with a knife; don't shake or pack down (except brown sugar, which is lightly packed). To measure liquids, use a **glass measuring cup** (1 cup/250 mL or 2 cup/500 mL) with metric marked on one side and imperial on the other.

TACO DIP

Everyone loves this taco-flavoured, layered dip and it's very easy to make.

8 oz	**cream cheese, softened**	**250 g**
½ cup	**sour cream**	**125 mL**
1 cup	**hot or mild salsa**	**250 mL**
½ cup	**chopped green onions**	**125 mL**
1 cup	**shredded iceberg lettuce**	**250 mL**
2	**tomatoes, chopped**	**2**
1 ½ cups	**shredded Cheddar cheese**	**375 mL**
	Tortilla chips	

1 In bowl, beat cream cheese and sour cream together until smooth. Spread evenly in bottom of 9-inch (23 cm) pie plate or shallow serving dish.

2 Spread salsa over cream cheese layer. Sprinkle evenly with onions, then lettuce, tomatoes and cheese.

3 Serve with tortilla chips. Serves 6 to 8 people.

HOT SHRIMP DIP

A deliciously different dip for raw vegetables, crackers, mini-pitas, bagel thins, soft breadsticks or small toasts. With a microwave, you can prepare this in about 5 minutes.

4 oz	**cream cheese, softened**	**125 g**
¼ cup	**mayonnaise**	**50 mL**
¼ cup	**chopped green onions**	**50 mL**
1	**clove garlic, minced**	**1**
2 tbsp	**lemon juice**	**25 mL**
2 tbsp	**tomato paste**	**25 mL**
1	**can (about 113 g) tiny shrimp**	**1**
	Pepper and salt	

1 In microwavable bowl, blend together cream cheese and mayonnaise.

2 Stir in onions, garlic, lemon juice and tomato paste. Blend in shrimp, mashing with a fork. Season to taste with pepper, and salt if needed.

3 Microwave on High for about 3 minutes or until very hot, stirring once halfway through. (Or heat in small casserole in 350°F/180°C oven for about 20 minutes.) Serves about 6 people.

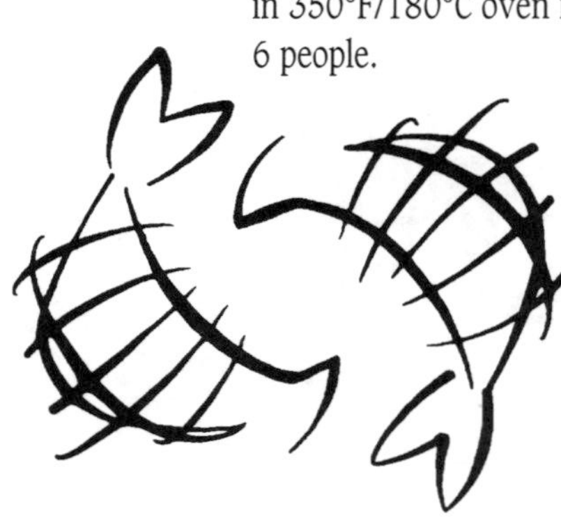

VEGGIE PLATTER WITH DIPS

Here's an easy, all-purpose dip recipe with variations that you can also use for chips, crackers or chicken wings. The Blue Cheese Dip is also good with veggies.

See page 18 for Blue Cheese Dip recipe.

SOUR CREAM & ONION DIP

For a low-fat dip, use light sour cream and light mayonnaise.

1 cup	**sour cream**	**250 mL**
½ cup	**mayonnaise**	**125 mL**
¼ cup	**finely chopped green onions**	**50 mL**
1	**clove garlic, minced**	**1**
	Salt and pepper to taste	

Mix all ingredients together. Cover and refrigerate at least one hour to blend flavours. Makes about 1 ½ cups (375 mL).

VARIATIONS

COTTAGE CHEESE DIP: Instead of sour cream and mayonnaise, use 1 cup (250 mL) creamed cottage cheese and ½ cup (125 mL) sour cream or plain yogurt; blend until smooth in blender or with electric mixer.

DILLED DIP: Reduce onions to 2 tbsp (25 mL). Add 2 tbsp (25 mL) chopped fresh dill or 2 tsp (10 mL) dried dillweed.

Vegetable Crudités

A big colourful platter of cut-up raw vegetables (called crudités) makes delicious, nutritious munchies. For 6 people, you will need about 8 cups (2 L) of prepared veggies. Choose a variety such as carrots, celery, zucchini and peppers (cut in sticks), broccoli and cauliflower florets, cucumber slices, green onions, radishes, cherry tomatoes, small mushrooms. Arrange on large platter with one or two dips.

NACHOS

A popular hot snack that couldn't be easier to make.

30 to 40	**tortilla chips**	**30 to 40**
½ cup	**hot taco sauce or salsa**	**125 mL**
2 cups	**shredded Cheddar *or* Monterey Jack cheese**	**500 mL**
	Sour cream	

1 Preheat oven to 400°F (200°C).

2 Arrange chips, just touching, in single layer on large shallow baking pan, pizza pan or ovenproof serving dish.

3 Spoon taco sauce evenly over chips. Sprinkle with cheese.

4 Bake for about 4 minutes or until cheese melts. Serve with sour cream for dipping if desired. Makes about 4 servings.

GUACAMOLE

This avocado dip is a favourite with corn chips, but also makes a good topping for nachos or fajitas.

2	**small ripe avocados**	**2**
1	**small tomato, seeded and chopped**	**1**
1 tbsp	**chopped fresh cilantro (coriander), optional**	**15 mL**
2 tbsp	**lime juice**	**25 mL**
1	**clove garlic, minced**	**1**
1	**jalapeño pepper, minced *or* dash hot pepper sauce**	**1**
	Salt and pepper to taste	

1 Peel and pit avocados; mash with fork until smooth or chunky as desired.

2 Add remaining ingredients. Cover with plastic wrap directly on the surface to prevent discolouration. Makes about 1 ½ cups (375 mL).

CHICKEN FAJITAS

Fajitas are soft tortillas wrapped around a spicy Tex-Mex filling.

In restaurants, fajitas are usually served in a sizzling pan. Everyone assembles their own, with toppings. You can do the same at a home party; have the vegetables sliced and the chicken marinating so you can cook the filling quickly just before serving.

¾ lb	**boneless, skinless chicken breasts**	**375 g**
2 tbsp	**lime juice**	**25 mL**
2 tbsp	**salsa**	**25 mL**
1	**clove garlic, minced**	**1**
1 tsp	**chili powder**	**5 mL**
½ tsp	**ground cumin**	**2 mL**
8	**flour tortillas**	**8**
2 tbsp	**olive oil**	**25 mL**
1	**large onion, sliced**	**1**
1	**green or red pepper, sliced into strips**	**1**
	Salt and pepper	
Toppings:	**salsa, sour cream, guacamole**	

See page 15 for Guacamole recipe.

1 Cut chicken into thin strips. Place in bowl. Add lime juice, salsa, garlic, chili powder and cumin; stir and set aside (refrigerate if not using right away).

2 Wrap tortillas (in stacks of 4) in foil; heat in 350°F (180°C) oven for 10 minutes or until hot.

3 Meanwhile, in large skillet over medium-high heat, heat oil. Sauté onions and peppers just until tender-crisp, about 3 minutes. Remove with slotted spoon and set aside.

4 Add chicken (and any juices in bowl) to skillet. Cook, stirring, until chicken is cooked through, about 3 minutes.

5 Return onions and peppers to pan. Mixture should be very moist; add a little more salsa if moisture is needed. Add salt and pepper to taste. Stir over high heat until very hot, about 1 minute.

6 Spoon chicken mixture down centre of hot tortillas. Add choice of toppings; roll up. Makes 8 fajitas (3 to 4 servings). Recipe may be doubled.

CRISPY WINGS WITH DIPS

Wings seem to be everyone's favourite party food. Baking is easier than deep-frying to make wings crisp.

2 ½ lbs	**chicken wings (about 20)**	**1.25 kg**
	Seasoned salt, pepper	

1 Cut off wing tips at joint; discard or use in stock. Cut remaining wings into two pieces at joint.

2 Preheat oven to 425°F (220°C). Arrange wings in single layer in greased shallow baking pan (preferably non-stick). Sprinkle wings on both sides with seasoned salt and pepper.

3 Bake for about 30 minutes or until crispy, turning them over halfway through. Serve hot, with dips (see below). Makes 4 to 6 servings.

BLUE CHEESE DIP

Combine ⅔ **cup (150 mL) sour cream,** ⅓ **cup (75 mL) mayonnaise** and **2 oz (50 g) crumbled blue cheese**; blend until smooth. Makes about 1 cup (250 mL).

HOT & SPICY DIP

Combine ½ **cup (125 mL) ketchup,** ¼ **cup (50 mL) honey, 2 tbsp (25 mL) lemon juice or vinegar** and ½ **tsp (2 mL) dried hot pepper flakes or dash of hot pepper sauce** (to taste). Microwave on High for 1 minute or until hot. Makes ¾ cup (175 mL).

HONEY-GARLIC CHICKEN WINGS

Coated with a spicy-sweet glaze, these make deliciously sticky finger food, or can be served as a main course with rice.

2 ½ lbs	**chicken wings (about 20)**	**1.25 kg**
	Salt and pepper	

Honey-Garlic Sauce:

½ cup	**soy sauce**	**125 mL**
½ cup	**liquid honey**	**125 mL**
2 tbsp	**ketchup**	**25 mL**
2	**cloves garlic, minced**	**2**
½ tsp	**powdered ginger**	**2 mL**

1 Cut off wing tips at joint; discard or use in stock. Cut remaining wings into two pieces at joint.

2 Preheat oven to 425°F (220°C). Arrange wings in single layer in greased shallow baking pan (preferably non-stick). Sprinkle wings on both sides with salt and pepper.

3 Bake for 15 minutes; drain off any liquid in pan.

4 HONEY-GARLIC SAUCE: Combine ingredients; pour over wings in pan.

5 Bake for about 30 minutes longer, turning wings over several times and brushing with sauce, until sauce thickens into a glaze and wings are well coated and browned. Makes about 6 servings.

BRUSCHETTA

Toasted Italian bread with a fresh tomato salad topping has become really popular in restaurants and makes a terrific party snack or pre-dinner appetizer.

About 8	**plum tomatoes or 3 large tomatoes**	**8**
2	**cloves garlic, minced**	**2**
2 tbsp	**chopped onion**	**25 mL**
2 tbsp	**chopped fresh basil**	**25 mL**
½ tsp	**dried oregano**	**2 mL**
3 tbsp	**good quality olive oil**	**45 mL**
	Salt and pepper	
8	**thick slices crusty Italian bread (about 4 in/10 cm diameter)**	**8**

1 Cut tomatoes in half; squeeze out seeds and juice. Chop finely; you should have about 2 cups (500 mL).

2 Combine with garlic, onion, basil, oregano and 1 tbsp (15 mL) of the olive oil. Season generously with salt and pepper to taste. Let stand at room temperature for about 1 hour; drain off liquid.

3 Toast bread under broiler (or on barbecue) until golden on both sides. Quickly brush one side of hot bread slices with remaining olive oil.

4 Spoon tomato mixture on top. Serve immediately. Makes about 4 servings (2 slices each).

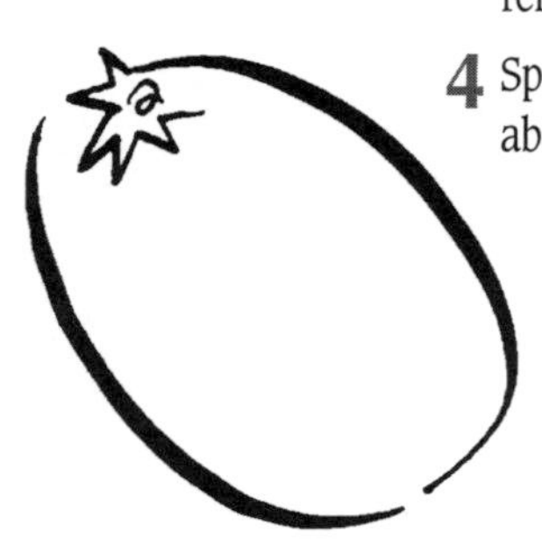

SPICED NUTS

A crisp spicy-sweet coating makes these popular as party nibbles or with after-dinner coffee. Wrapped in a pretty package, they make great little gifts from your kitchen. They also look nice mixed with plain peanuts.

1	**egg white**	**1**
2 cups	**blanched almonds, peanuts, pecan halves or mixed nuts**	**500 mL**
½ cup	**granulated sugar**	**125 mL**
2 tsp	**cinnamon**	**10 mL**
¼ tsp	**each: nutmeg, allspice and ginger**	**1 mL**
½ tsp	**salt**	**2 mL**

1 Preheat oven to 300°F (150°C).

2 In bowl, beat egg white with fork until frothy. Add nuts and toss until coated.

3 In large bowl, combine sugar, spices and salt. Add nuts and toss until well-coated.

4 Spread nuts out in single layer on greased or non-stick baking sheet.

5 Bake for about 30 minutes, stirring occasionally, until nuts are dried and crispy. Let cool. Makes 2 cups (500 mL).

Trail Mix

Mix up a batch of this high-energy snack for hiking, biking, or cramming at exam time. Check out bulk food stores for your favourite ingredients, and custom-mix to taste. Example: About **½ cup (125 mL) each** of **peanuts or mixed nuts, raisins, dried apricots or bananas, rolled oats** and **sunflower seeds,** plus **¼ cup (50 mL) coconut and sesame seeds.** Makes about 3 cups (750 mL). Store in tightly covered container.

EGG SALAD SANDWICHES

Use this filling for sandwiches, or chop the ingredients finely and use as a spread with crackers, or chop in larger pieces for a chunky salad.

3	**hard-cooked eggs, coarsely chopped**	**3**
2	**green onions, chopped**	**2**
1	**stalk celery, chopped**	**1**
	Mayonnaise	
	Salt and pepper	

1. In a bowl, mix together eggs, onions and celery.
2. Add enough mayonnaise to moisten. Season with salt and pepper to taste. Makes enough for 2 or 3 sandwiches.

VARIATIONS

TUNA, SALMON, SHRIMP, TURKEY OR CHICKEN SALAD SANDWICHES: Instead of eggs, use 1 can of tuna, salmon or shrimp (drained) or 1 cup of chopped cooked turkey or chicken.

OPEN FACE SANDWICHES: Top firm-textured slices of bread with lettuce and/or alfalfa sprouts; mound filling on top.

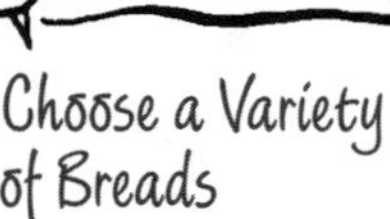

Choose a Variety of Breads

Bakeries and supermarkets offer varieties of breads and buns of different flavours, shapes and sizes to make your sandwiches interesting: wholewheat, oat, rye and mixed grains of every kind, crusty white loaves and rolls, kaisers, croissants, bagels, pitas. Remember to choose wholegrains often.

HOT SANDWICHES

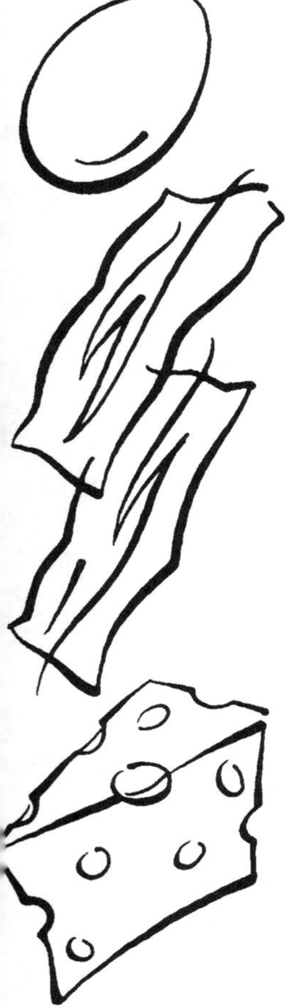

TOASTED WESTERN SANDWICHES

These are called Denver sandwiches in western Canada. For 2 sandwiches, chop **3 slices of bacon**; cook in non-stick skillet over medium heat until nearly crisp. Drain fat. Add **2 chopped green onions** and cook until softened. In small bowl, beat **4 eggs**; pour into skillet and cook until golden underneath and nearly set on top. Cut in half and turn each half over with large metal spatula; cook briefly until underside is golden. Sprinkle with **pepper**. Sandwich egg between **toast slices**.

GRILLED CHEESE SANDWICHES

Butter bread slices on one side only. With buttered side out, make sandwiches with **sliced Cheddar or Swiss cheese**. Place sandwiches in non-stick skillet over medium heat; cook until golden brown underneath; turn over and cook until browned underneath and cheese is melted.

FRENCH TOASTED SANDWICHES

These are called Croque-Monsieur in France. For 2 sandwiches, spread **4 slices of white bread** very lightly with **Dijon mustard**. Make into 2 sandwiches, each filled with **1 slice Swiss cheese** and **1 slice cooked ham**. In shallow dish, beat together **2 eggs** and **¼ cup (50 mL) milk**. Dip sandwiches in egg mixture, turning to coat both sides. In non-stick skillet over medium heat, melt **2 tsp (10 mL) butter**. Add sandwiches and cook until golden brown underneath. Add another **1 tsp (5 mL) butter** to skillet; turn sandwiches and brown the other side.

COUNTRY KITCHEN PEA SOUP

This is similar to old-fashioned French-Canadian pea soup, but easier because it uses split peas instead of whole peas (which have to soak overnight before cooking). Make it when you'll be home for a while to enjoy the delicious smell wafting from the simmering soup pot.

2 cups	**dried split peas**	**500 mL**
6 cups	**water**	**1.5 L**
1	**piece salt pork (4 oz/125 g)**	**1**
1	**large onion, chopped**	**1**
½ cup	**chopped celery**	**125 mL**
½ cup	**chopped carrots**	**125 mL**
1	**bay leaf**	**1**
½ tsp	**salt**	**2 mL**
½ tsp	**dried savory**	**2 mL**
¼ tsp	**pepper**	**1 mL**
	Salt and pepper	

1 In large saucepan, combine all ingredients. Bring to boil; reduce heat and simmer, covered, for 1 to 1 ½ hours or until peas are tender.

2 Remove salt pork and bay leaf. To give soup creamier texture, remove about one quarter of the soup from pot and purée in blender or food processor; return mixture to soup. (Or just mash soup in the pot slightly with potato masher.)

3 Chop salt pork finely (discard fat) and return it to the soup.

4 Add salt and pepper to taste. Makes about 6 servings. This soup is good reheated; add a little water if too thick.

LENTIL VEGETABLE SOUP

Lentils contribute protein and great flavour to meatless meals. This soup can be varied by adding different spices or herbs, dried beans or any vegetables you wish. Minestrone is similar, with pasta added.

2 tbsp	**olive oil**	**25 mL**
½ cup	**finely chopped onion**	**125 mL**
¼ cup	**each: finely chopped celery, carrot, green pepper**	**50 mL**
1	**clove garlic, minced**	**1**
1	**can (14 oz/398 mL) tomatoes**	**1**
½ cup	**dried lentils, rinsed**	**125 mL**
2 cups	**chicken or vegetable stock**	**500 mL**
¼ tsp	**each: oregano and basil**	**1 mL**
	Salt and pepper	

1. In large saucepan over medium heat, heat oil. Add onion, celery, carrot, green pepper and garlic. Cover and cook, stirring often, until softened but not browned, about 5 minutes.
2. Add tomatoes, breaking them up with back of spoon or potato masher.
3. Add lentils, chicken stock, oregano and basil.
4. Cover and simmer until lentils are tender, about 45 minutes; stir occasionally. Add a little more stock or water if too thick.
5. Season to taste with salt and pepper. Makes about 4 servings.

Minestrone

Instead of lentils, add **½ cup (125 mL) cooked or canned kidney beans, ¼ cup (50 mL) uncooked macaroni** and **1 cup (250 mL) shredded cabbage.**

Lentil Soup/ Minestrone with Sausage

Lightly brown **¼ lb (125 g) sliced or crumbled Italian sausage** in the saucepan before adding the vegetables.

FRENCH ONION SOUP

Your friends will think they're in a French bistro when you serve them this gorgeous soup. It's surprisingly easy to make.

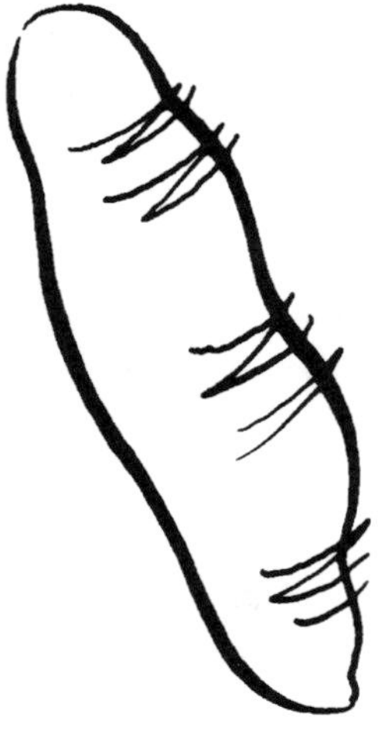

2 tbsp	**butter**	**25 mL**
3 cups	**thinly sliced onions**	**750 mL**
1	**clove garlic, minced**	**1**
½ tsp	**salt**	**2 mL**
½ tsp	**sugar**	**2 mL**
2 tbsp	**all-purpose flour**	**25 mL**
2	**cans (10 oz/284 mL each) beef broth**	**2**
2 cups	**water**	**500 mL**
	Pepper and salt to taste	
Topping:		
4	**thick slices French bread (about 3 in/8 cm diameter)**	**4**
1 cup	**shredded Swiss or Gruyère cheese**	**250 mL**
¼ cup	**grated Parmesan cheese**	**50 mL**

1 In large heavy saucepan over medium-high heat, melt butter. Add onions, garlic, salt and sugar. Cook, stirring often, for about 20 minutes or until dark golden brown.

2 Stir in flour. Add beef broth and water. Bring to boil, stirring; reduce heat, cover and simmer for about 30 minutes. Add pepper, and salt if needed.

3 TOPPING: Toast bread under broiler until crisp and golden brown on both sides. Pour hot soup into ovenproof onion soup bowls (about 4 in/10 cm diameter). Float bread on top. Top with shredded cheese and sprinkle with Parmesan. Place under broiler until bubbly and lightly browned. Makes 4 servings.

FISH CHOWDER

Enjoy a taste of the Maritimes with this traditional chowder or any of the seafood variations.

2 tbsp	**butter**	**25 mL**
1 cup	**chopped onions**	**250 mL**
¼ cup	**chopped celery**	**50 mL**
2 tbsp	**all-purpose flour**	**25 mL**
	Salt and pepper	
3 cups	**water**	**750 mL**
2 cups	**diced potatoes**	**500 mL**
1 lb	**cod or other white fillets (fresh or frozen)**	**500 g**
2 cups	**milk *or* light cream**	**500 mL**

1 In large heavy saucepan over medium heat, melt butter. Add onion and celery; cook until softened. Stir in flour; sprinkle lightly with salt and pepper. Stir in water.

2 Add potatoes. Bring to boil; reduce heat, cover and simmer until potatoes are tender, about 10 minutes, stirring occasionally.

3 Cut fish in small pieces. Add to pot; cover and simmer for 5 minutes.

4 Add milk; heat gently until very hot; do not boil. Add salt and pepper to taste. Makes 4 to 6 servings.

VARIATIONS

SEAFOOD CHOWDER: Instead of cod, use about 2 cups (500 mL) scallops, lobster or mixed seafood cut in bite-size pieces.

CLAM CHOWDER: Instead of cod, use 2 cans (5 oz/142 g each) clams. Replace part of the water with juice drained from clams; add clams after adding the milk.

QUICK BORSCHT

Hearty borscht is a traditional favourite from eastern Europe, and many different versions are made in Canadian kitchens. This non-traditional variation has great flavour and beautiful colour and is easy to make with canned beets.

1 tbsp	**butter**	**15 mL**
1	**onion, chopped**	**1**
1	**clove garlic, minced**	**1**
1 cup	**shredded red cabbage**	**250 mL**
1	**can (10 oz/284 mL) diced beets, undrained**	**1**
1	**can (14 oz/398 mL) tomatoes**	**1**
1	**can (10 oz/284 mL) beef broth**	**1**
1 cup	**water**	**250 mL**
2 tbsp	**red wine vinegar**	**25 mL**
½ tsp	**granulated sugar**	**2 mL**
1 tsp	**dried dillweed**	**5 mL**
	Salt and pepper to taste	
Garnish:	**Sour cream**	

1 In large heavy saucepan over medium heat, melt butter. Add onion and cook until softened. Add garlic and cabbage; cook, stirring, until cabbage is wilted.

2 Add remaining ingredients except salt and pepper. Cover and simmer for about 30 minutes; season to taste.

3 Garnish each serving with a dollop of sour cream, if desired. Makes about 4 servings.

GOLDEN HARVEST SOUP

This is a beautiful smooth soup for a crisp fall or winter evening.

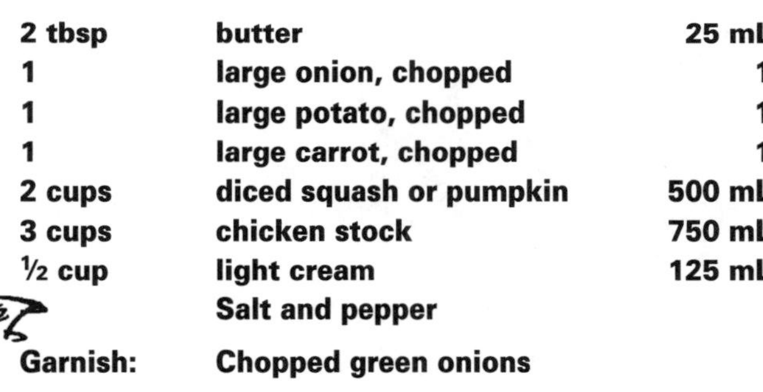

2 tbsp	**butter**	**25 mL**
1	**large onion, chopped**	**1**
1	**large potato, chopped**	**1**
1	**large carrot, chopped**	**1**
2 cups	**diced squash or pumpkin**	**500 mL**
3 cups	**chicken stock**	**750 mL**
½ cup	**light cream**	**125 mL**
	Salt and pepper	
Garnish:	**Chopped green onions**	

1 In large heavy saucepan over medium heat, melt butter. Add onions and cook until softened but not browned.

2 Add potatoes, carrots, squash and stock.

3 Cover and simmer for about 20 minutes or until vegetables are soft.

4 In food processor or blender, purée soup until very smooth. Return to saucepan.

5 Stir in cream and heat until very hot but not boiling. Season to taste with salt and pepper.

6 Garnish each serving with a sprinkle of green onion. Makes about 4 servings.

Chicken Stock

When recipes call for chicken stock, canned chicken broth is fine if you don't have homemade. You can also make stock from bouillon cubes or powder, but they are usually very salty so be sure to taste and adjust salt in recipe.

GREEN SALAD & DRESSINGS

For a simple tossed green salad, use one kind or a variet of mixed greens:

romaine, Boston, butter or leaf lettuce, spinach;
red leaf lettuce or radicchio (for colour);
iceberg lettuce (for crunch);
curly endive, escarole, watercress (for sharper flavour)

Wash greens as soon as you get them home; dry in salad spinner or on paper towels; store in plastic bags in refrigerator To make salad, tear (don't cut) greens into small pieces; plac in salad bowl. Just before serving, toss with dressing (just enough to coat the leaves). Any other vegetables such as tomatoes or cucumbers should be added just before serving.

THOUSAND ISLAND DRESSING

½ cup	**mayonnaise**	**125 m**
2 tbsp	**ketchup *or* chili sauce**	**25 m**
2 tbsp	**green pickle relish**	**25 m**
	Milk (optional)	

1 Combine mayonnaise, ketchup or chili sauce, and green pickle relish.

2 Thin with a little milk if desired. Makes about ¾ cup (175 mL).

CLASSIC VINAIGRETTE DRESSING

2 tbsp	**red or white wine vinegar**	**25 mL**
½ tsp	**Dijon mustard (optional)**	**2 mL**
½ tsp	**salt**	**2 mL**
	Freshly ground pepper	
6-8 tbsp	**olive oil or vegetable oil**	**75-100 mL**

1 In a small bowl, whisk together vinegar, mustard (optional), salt and pepper.

2 Gradually whisk in 6 tbsp (75 mL) oil.

3 Taste the dressing on a lettuce leaf; if the flavour is too sharp add 2 tbsp (25 mL) more oil. Makes about ½ cup (125 mL).

VARIATIONS

GARLIC VINAIGRETTE: Add **one crushed garlic clove** to the vinegar.

HERBED VINAIGRETTE: Add **1 tsp (15 mL) dried** or **1 tbsp (15 mL) minced fresh herbs: basil, tarragon, chives, parsley or mixture.**

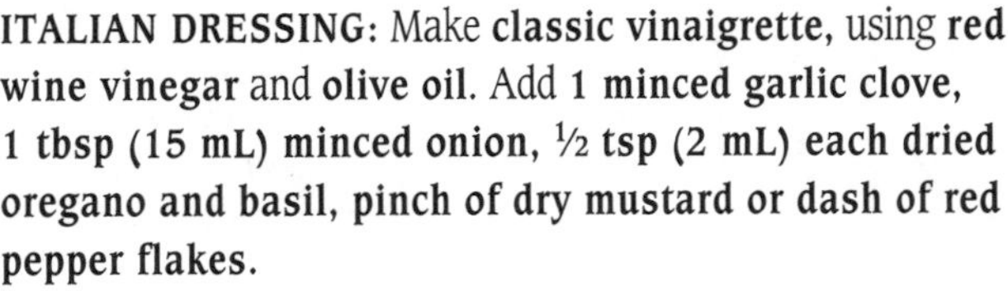

ITALIAN DRESSING: Make **classic vinaigrette,** using **red wine vinegar** and **olive oil.** Add **1 minced garlic clove, 1 tbsp (15 mL) minced onion, ½ tsp (2 mL) each dried oregano and basil, pinch of dry mustard or dash of red pepper flakes.**

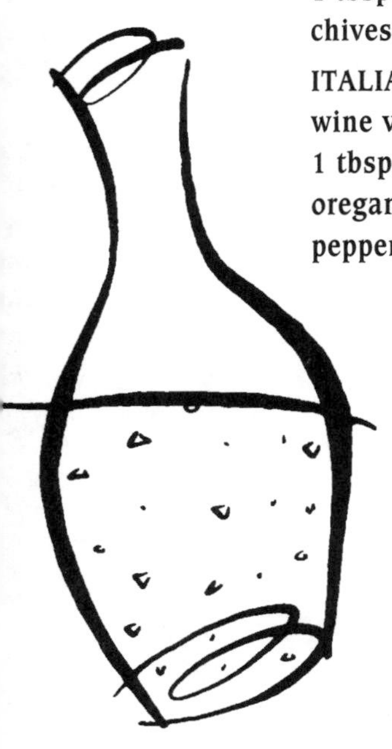

CAESAR SALAD

This streamlined version uses an easy blender dressin

Romaine lettuce (one head per 3-4 servings)
Easy Caesar Dressing (recipe below)
Freshly grated Parmesan cheese
Croutons

1 Tear romaine into bite-size pieces. Place in salad bowl.

2 Toss with just enough dressing to coat leaves lightly. Ad
Parmesan to taste; toss again.

3 Top with croutons.

EASY CAESAR DRESSING

This is also good on spinach or pasta salads.

1	**egg** (see note)	
2 tbsp	**red wine vinegar**	**25 m**
1 tbsp	**lemon juice**	**15 m**
2	**cloves garlic**	
2	**anchovy fillets or 1 tsp (5 mL) anchovy paste**	
1 tsp	**Dijon mustard**	**5 m**
½ tsp	**Worcestershire sauce**	**2 m**
¼ tsp	**salt**	**1 m**
¼ tsp	**pepper**	**1 m**
2 tbsp	**grated Parmesan cheese**	**25 m**
⅔ cup	**olive oil**	**150 m**

1 In electric blender, combine all ingredients except oil; blend about 30 seconds until smooth.

2 With blender running, add oil gradually in steady stream.

3 Transfer to covered jar; store in refrigerator up to 3 days. Makes about 1 cup (250 mL)/about 8 servings.

NOTE: If you prefer not to use raw egg, add 2 tbsp (25 mL) mayonnaise instea
This recipe may be halved.

MEDITERRANEAN PASTA SALAD

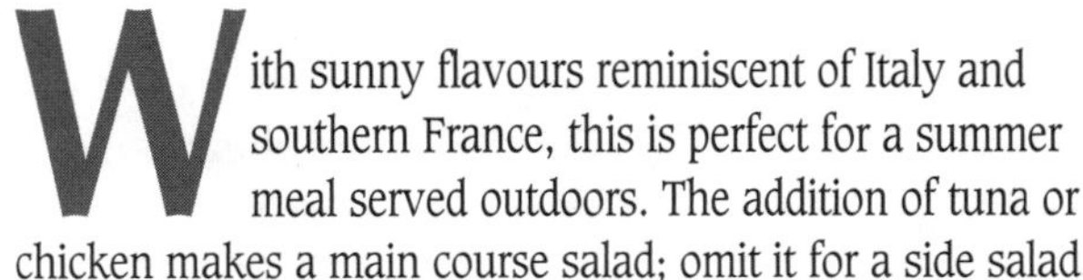

With sunny flavours reminiscent of Italy and southern France, this is perfect for a summer meal served outdoors. The addition of tuna or chicken makes a main course salad; omit it for a side salad.

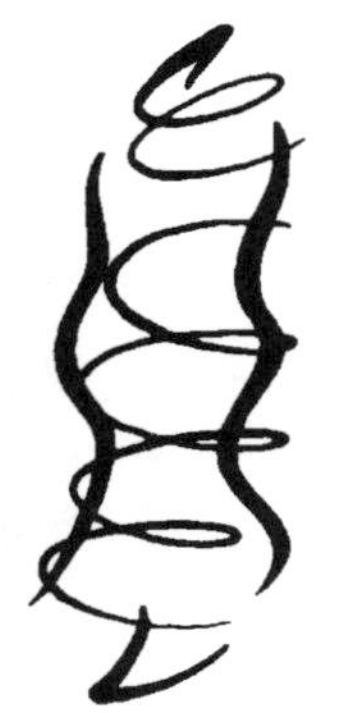

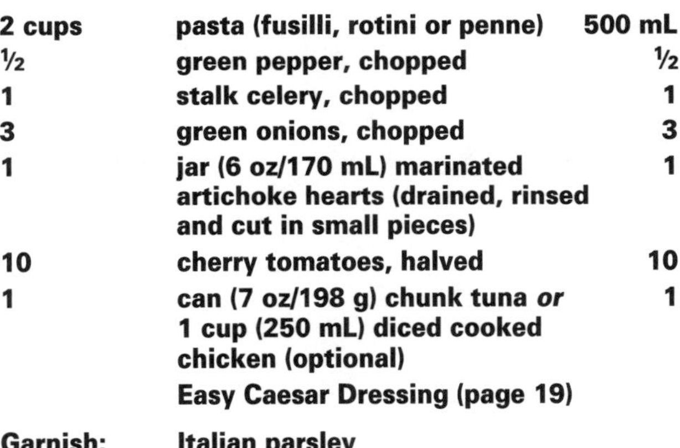

2 cups	**pasta (fusilli, rotini or penne)**	**500 mL**
½	**green pepper, chopped**	**½**
1	**stalk celery, chopped**	**1**
3	**green onions, chopped**	**3**
1	**jar (6 oz/170 mL) marinated artichoke hearts (drained, rinsed and cut in small pieces)**	**1**
10	**cherry tomatoes, halved**	**10**
1	**can (7 oz/198 g) chunk tuna *or* 1 cup (250 mL) diced cooked chicken (optional)**	**1**
	Easy Caesar Dressing (page 19)	
Garnish:	**Italian parsley**	

1 In large pot of boiling salted water, cook pasta until tender but firm, about 10 minutes. Drain into colander and rinse under cold running water; drain well.

2 In large bowl, combine pasta, green pepper, celery, onions, artichokes and tomatoes. Add tuna or chicken, if using.

3 Add just enough dressing to coat lightly (about ¼ cup/50 mL); mix gently.

4 Spoon salad into serving bowl.

5 GARNISH with parsley. Makes 4 to 6 servings.

POTATO SALAD

A good potato salad is a very satisfying dish for simpl summer meals. Use new potatoes for best texture.

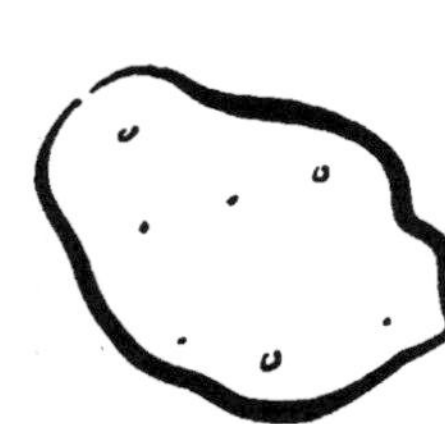

6	**medium potatoes**	
2 tbsp	**each: vegetable oil and white vinegar**	**25 m**
1	**small onion, chopped**	
4	**green onions, chopped**	
½ cup	**chopped celery**	**125 m**
4	**hard-cooked eggs**	
¾ cup	**(approx.) mayonnaise**	**175 m**
	Salt and pepper	
	Sliced radishes	
	Parsley sprigs	

1 Peel potatoes and cut in half. Cover with salted water in large saucepan. Boil until tender but still firm, about 20 minutes. Drain; let potatoes cool until just slightly warm.

2 Cut potatoes into small cubes and place in large bowl. Drizzle with oil and vinegar; toss. Add onions, celery and two of the eggs (cut up).

3 Add enough mayonnaise to coat potatoes well. Season with salt and pepper to taste, mixing thoroughly. Cover and refrigerate at least 2 hours.

4 Spoon into serving bowl. Cut remaining eggs into slices. Garnish top of salad with egg and radish slices and parsley. Makes 4 to 6 servings.

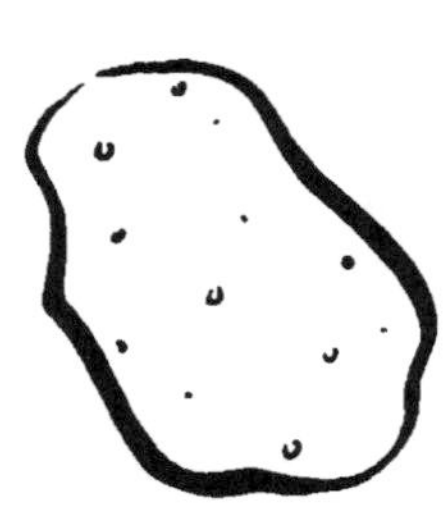

MAKE-AHEAD COLE SLAW

This is a tangy slaw that everyone likes; it will keep up to a week in the fridge.

6 cups	**shredded cabbage**	**1.5 L**
1	**medium carrot, grated**	**1**
1	**small onion, chopped**	**1**
½ cup	**white vinegar**	**125 mL**
¼ cup	**granulated sugar**	**50 mL**
¼ cup	**vegetable oil**	**50 mL**
1 tsp	**salt**	**5 mL**
½ tsp	**celery seed**	**2 mL**
dash	**pepper**	**dash**

1 Shred cabbage finely with large sharp knife; place in large bowl. Add carrots and onions.

2 In glass measuring cup, combine remaining ingredients; microwave on High about 1 minute or until boiling; stir to dissolve sugar. (Or heat in small saucepan on stove.)

3 Pour hot dressing over cabbage mixture; stir to mix well. Cover and chill. Makes 6 to 8 servings.

MIXED BEAN SALAD

A sweet-and-sour dressing enhances this popular salad. It will keep several days in the fridge. The canned green and yellow beans can be replaced with fresh beans cooked tender-crisp. The recipe is easily doubled, using one can (14 oz/398 mL) of each kind of bean.

1 cup	**each: canned cut green beans, yellow wax beans, red kidney beans, chickpeas**	**250 mL**
½ cup	**chopped celery**	**125 mL**
¼ cup	**chopped onion**	**50 mL**
¼ cup	**chopped green pepper**	**50 mL**
¼ cup	**white vinegar**	**50 mL**
¼ cup	**vegetable oil**	**50 mL**
2 tbsp	**granulated sugar**	**25 mL**
½ tsp	**salt**	**2 mL**
¼ tsp	**pepper**	**1 mL**

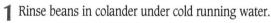

1 Rinse beans in colander under cold running water.

2 In large bowl, combine beans, celery, onion and green pepper.

3 Whisk together vinegar, oil, sugar, salt and pepper. Pour over bean mixture and mix well.

4 Cover and chill at least 3 hours. Drain before serving. Makes about 4 servings.

MARINATED VEGGIE SALAD

This is a very attractive, healthful vegetable dish and salad all in one.

1 cup	**sliced carrots**	**250 mL**
1 cup	**cut green beans**	**250 mL**
1 cup	**broccoli florets**	**250 mL**
1 cup	**cauliflower florets**	**250 mL**
½ cup	**red or green pepper strips**	**125 mL**
½ cup	**sliced celery**	**125 mL**
Marinade:		
½ cup	**olive oil**	**125 mL**
¼ cup	**white wine vinegar**	**50 mL**
2 tbsp	**lemon juice**	**25 mL**
1	**clove garlic, minced**	**1**
½ tsp	**salt**	**2 mL**
¼ tsp	**pepper**	**1 mL**
2 tbsp	**chopped parsley**	**25 mL**

1 In saucepan of boiling, lightly salted water, cook carrots, beans, broccoli and cauliflower until nearly tender but still crisp (about 4 minutes for carrots, 2 minutes for the others). Or microwave on High for 1 to 2 minutes each.

2 As soon as vegetables are cooked tender-crisp, drain and plunge them into bowl of cold water.

3 Drain vegetables in colander, then place in large bowl. Add peppers and celery.

4 MARINADE: In small bowl, combine all ingredients. Pour over vegetables; stir well. Taste and add salt if needed.

5 Cover and refrigerate for 1 to 2 hours, stirring occasionally. Makes about 4 servings.

Cooking Tip

When cooking a variety of vegetables, it's best to cook each one separately because cooking times will vary. Plunging them into cold water afterwards will keep their colour bright.

GREEK SALAD

Greek salad does not have lettuce, but you could add the same ingredients to a tossed salad of lettuce, romaine or mixed greens.

3	**medium tomatoes**	**3**
1	**seedless cucumber, peeled**	**1**
1	**small red onion, chopped**	**1**
½ cup	**black olives (preferably Kalamata)**	**125 mL**
4 oz	**feta cheese**	**125 g**
Dressing:		
⅔ cup	**olive oil**	**150 mL**
2 tbsp	**red wine vinegar**	**25 mL**
1 tbsp	**lemon juice**	**15 mL**
1	**clove garlic, minced**	**1**
2 tsp	**dried oregano**	**10 mL**
½ tsp	**salt**	**2 mL**
	Freshly ground pepper	

1 DRESSING: In small bowl, whisk ingredients together.

2 Cut tomatoes and cucumber into chunks. Combine with onion in large bowl. Add enough dressing to coat the vegetables.

3 Spoon salad onto large platter or shallow bowl. Scatter olives on top. Crumble feta cheese coarsely and sprinkle over salad. Makes about 4 servings.

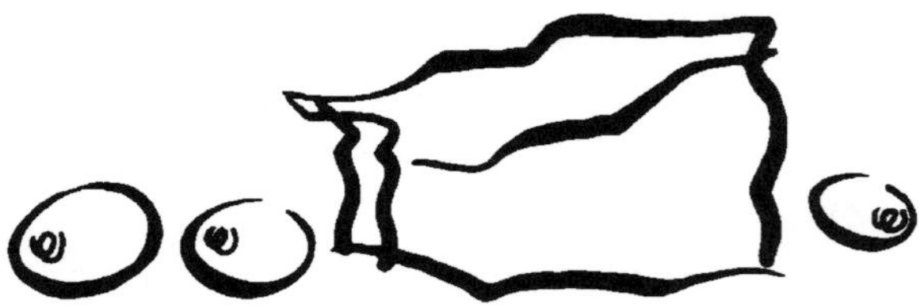

TOMATOES AND MOZZARELLA WITH BASIL

This is a beautiful salad for a hot summer day when garden tomatoes and fresh basil are at their peak. Be sure to use best quality mozzarella and olive oil.

½ lb	**fresh mozzarella cheese**	**250 g**
4	**ripe red tomatoes**	**4**
⅓ cup	**chopped fresh basil**	**75 mL**
Dressing:		
2 tbsp	**balsamic or wine vinegar**	**30 mL**
¼ tsp	**salt**	**1 mL**
	Freshly ground pepper	
6 tbsp	**olive oil**	**90 mL**

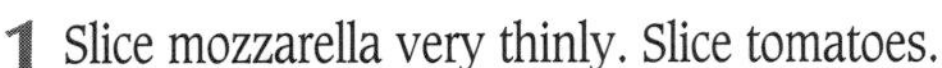

1 Slice mozzarella very thinly. Slice tomatoes.

2 On large platter, arrange alternate slices of mozzarella and tomatoes, slightly overlapping. Sprinkle with basil.

3 DRESSING: Whisk together all ingredients. Drizzle over mozzarella and tomatoes. Let stand at room temperature for 30 minutes. Serve with crusty Italian bread. Makes 4 to 6 servings.

VARIATION

TOMATO SALAD WITH BASIL: Omit mozzarella. Arrange tomatoes on platter and scatter with Spanish onion (cut in rings or chopped). If fresh basil is not available, use chopped parsley; add 1 tbsp (15 mL) dried basil to the dressing.

FRUIT SALAD BOWL

Beautiful and delicious for brunch or a summer dessert. Use any combination of fruit in season: sliced peaches or mangoes, orange sections, strawberries, blueberries, raspberries, melon cubes, seedless grapes, sliced kiwifruit or bananas.

4 cups	**mixed fresh fruit**	**1 L**
2 cups	**orange juice**	**500 mL**
¼ cup	**lime or lemon juice**	**50 mL**
	Sugar to taste	
	Fresh mint	

1 In glass serving bowl, combine fruit. (If using kiwi or bananas, add just before serving.)

2 Pour orange and lime juices over fruit. Stir in sugar to taste (fruit sugar dissolves quickly).

3 Cover and refrigerate up to one day. Garnish top with sprigs of mint.

4 To serve, spoon fruit and its juice into stemmed glasses; use small spoons for the fruit and sip the juice. Makes 4 to 6 servings.

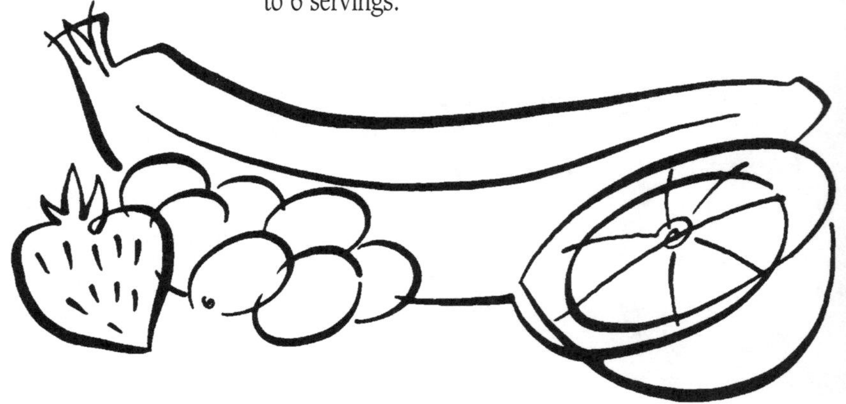

BAKED POTATOES WITH TOPPINGS

A baked potato with a great-tasting topping is ready in minutes in the microwave and makes a satisfying, nutritious supper; just add a salad. Make toppings while potatoes are baking in oven or during standing time after microwaving. Just before serving, cut a deep cross in top of each baked potato; squeeze lightly to open. Spoon topping over potato.

Baked Potatoes

Use large baking potatoes; scrub well, then prick several times with a fork.

TO MICROWAVE: Place on paper towel; microwave on High until just tender, about 4 minutes for one potato, 7 minutes for two, 10 minutes for three; turn potatoes once during cooking. Let stand 5 minutes.

TO OVEN-BAKE: In regular oven or toaster oven, bake at 400°F (200°C) for about 50 minutes, or at 350°F/180°C for 60-70 minutes, or until tender.

ITALIAN SAUSAGE, PEPPER AND TOMATO TOPPING

Cut **one small green pepper** into strips; microwave in small covered dish for 1½ minutes on High or until tender. Add **½ cup (125 mL) chunky tomato or thick pasta sauce** and **1 sliced cooked Italian sausage**; cover and microwave for 1 minute or until hot. Makes enough for 2 or 3 potatoes. For ***Spicy Mexican Topping***, use hot or mild salsa instead of pasta sauce.

CHEESE, HAM AND BROCCOLI TOPPING

In small covered dish, microwave **1 cup (250 mL) coarsely chopped broccoli** for 1½ minutes on High or until tender. Add **½ cup (125 mL) diced ham** and **1 cup (250 mL) shredded Cheddar cheese**. Cover and microwave for 1 minute or until cheese is melted. Makes enough for 2 or 3 potatoes.

OVEN-BAKED FRENCH FRIES

This method is much easier than deep-frying and produces crisp fries much lower in fat.

4	**large potatoes**	**4**
2 tbsp	**vegetable oil**	**25 mL**
	Salt	

1 Preheat oven to 450°F (230°C).

2 Peel potatoes and cut into sticks ½-inch (1 cm) thick. Pat dry with paper towels. Place in large bowl; toss with oil until coated. Spread in single layer on baking sheet (preferably non-stick).

3 Bake for about 20 minutes or until crisp and golden brown; turn them over halfway through baking. Sprinkle lightly with salt. Makes about 4 servings.

VARIATION

PARMESAN POTATOES: Cut unpeeled potatoes into ¼-inch (.5 cm) slices. Toss with oil and bake as for Oven-Baked French Fries, but after turning them over halfway through baking, sprinkle lightly with grated Parmesan cheese.

TOMATO-ZUCCHINI SAUTE

A tasty, colourful vegetable dish that takes only 5 minutes to make.

1 tbsp	**butter**	**15 mL**
1 tbsp	**olive oil**	**15 mL**
2	**small zucchini, sliced**	**2**
1 cup	**cherry tomatoes**	**250 mL**
1	**clove garlic, minced**	**1**
1 tbsp	**chopped parsley**	**15 mL**
½ tsp	**dried rosemary or basil**	**2 mL**
	Salt and pepper	

1 In large skillet over medium heat, melt butter with oil. Add zucchini and cook, stirring, until nearly tender, about 3 minutes.

2 Add tomatoes, garlic, parsley and rosemary. Cook, stirring gently, for about 2 minutes or just until tomatoes are softened and hot (if overcooked, they will collapse or break). Add salt and pepper to taste. Makes about 3 servings.

GREEN BEANS WITH ALMONDS

Green beans are easily dressed up with crunchy almonds (or you could use pine nuts instead). Sautéed mushrooms are another nice addition to either green beans or peas.

¾ lb	**fresh green beans**	**375 g**
¼ cup	**slivered almonds**	**50 mL**
1 tbsp	**butter**	**15 mL**
1	**small clove garlic, finely minced**	**1**
	Salt and pepper	

1. Trim ends from beans; leave beans whole or cut diagonally into pieces.
2. Bring saucepan of lightly salted water to full boil. Add beans and cook uncovered just until tender-crisp, about 3 minutes. Drain. (If making ahead, rinse under cold water to keep them bright green.)
3. In large skillet over medium heat, melt butter. Add almonds; stir until lightly browned. Add garlic (do not brown).
4. Add beans to skillet; toss until hot. Season with salt and pepper to taste. Makes about 3 servings.

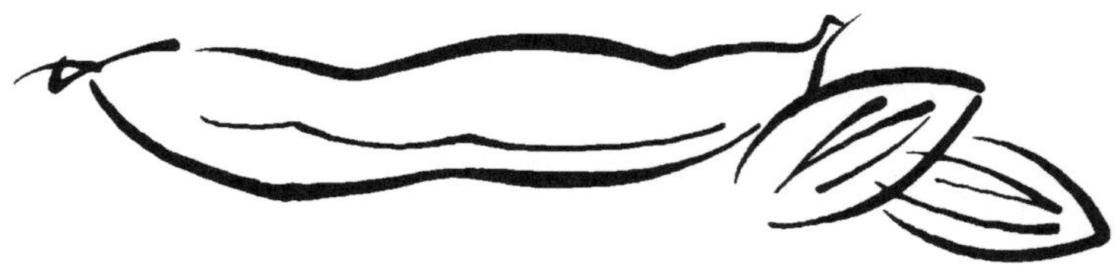

ORANGE-GLAZED CARROTS OR SWEET POTATOES

A shiny glaze brightens up the flavour and colour of orange vegetables; these are both good with roast pork, chicken or turkey.

4	**large carrots *or* sweet potatoes**	**4**
1 tbsp	**butter**	**15 mL**
2 tbsp	**packed brown sugar**	**25 mL**
2 tbsp	**frozen orange juice, thawed and undiluted**	**25 mL**

1 Peel vegetables and cut into thick slices. Cook in saucepan of boiling salted water about 10 minutes, or until tender but still firm. (Or place in covered dish with a little water, and microwave on High about 6 minutes.)

2 In large skillet over medium-high heat, melt butter. Stir in brown sugar and orange juice until melted and smooth. Add drained vegetables; cook, stirring and spooning sauce over vegetables, until hot and glazed, about 2 minutes. Makes about 4 servings.

BROCCOLI WITH CHEESE SAUCE

This is nutritious, delicious and very easy to make, especially with a microwave oven.

1	**bunch fresh broccoli (about 1 lb/500 g)**	**1**
	Microwave Cheese Sauce (recipe on page 54)	

To Cook on Stovetop:

Cook broccoli in a large pot of boiling, lightly salted water or in a steamer. While it's cooking, make **Stovetop Cheese Sauce** (recipe on page 54).

1 Wash broccoli; trim stalks and remove leaves. Peel stalks with a vegetable peeler or paring knife. Cut thick part of stalks into small pieces. Cut rest of broccoli into medium-sized florets.

2 Place broccoli in microwavable dish. Add about 2 tbsp/ 25 mL water (don't add salt). Cover with lid or plastic wrap. Microwave on High for 6 to 8 minutes or just until tender-crisp. (If your microwave doesn't have a turntable, rotate dish or stir twice during cooking.)

3 Prepare *Microwave Cheese Sauce* (you can combine the ingredients while broccoli is cooking; then let broccoli stand, tightly covered to keep hot, while you microwave the sauce).

4 Drain broccoli well and top with cheese sauce. Makes 4 to 6 servings. (For 2 to 3 servings, cut recipe in half.)

VARIATIONS

CAULIFLOWER WITH CHEESE SAUCE: Use cauliflower instead of broccoli. Or use a combination of broccoli and cauliflower.

TOMATOES PROVENÇALE

Bright red tomatoes with a crisp savoury topping are delicious as well as beautiful. To make the bread crumbs, just cut or crumble slightly dry bread into coarse crumbs.

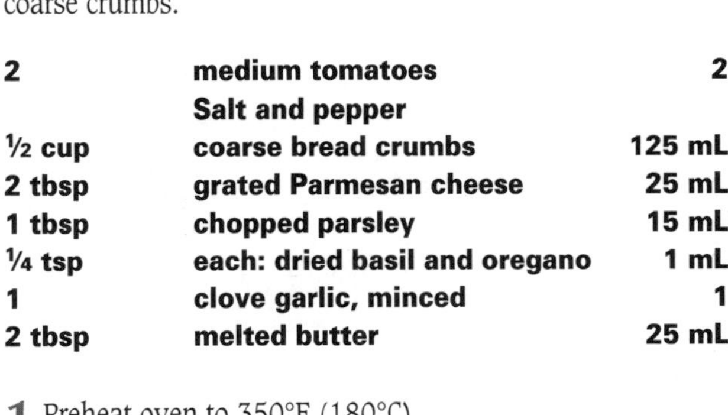

2	**medium tomatoes**	**2**
	Salt and pepper	
½ cup	**coarse bread crumbs**	**125 mL**
2 tbsp	**grated Parmesan cheese**	**25 mL**
1 tbsp	**chopped parsley**	**15 mL**
¼ tsp	**each: dried basil and oregano**	**1 mL**
1	**clove garlic, minced**	**1**
2 tbsp	**melted butter**	**25 mL**

1. Preheat oven to 350°F (180°C).
2. Cut tomatoes in half; gently squeeze out seeds and juice. Sprinkle lightly with salt and pepper.
3. In small bowl, combine bread crumbs, Parmesan, parsley, basil and oregano; toss with butter.
4. Place tomato halves in small baking dish. Spoon crumb mixture generously on top of each.
5. Bake for 20 minutes or until tomatoes are tender and topping is golden brown. Makes 2 to 4 servings. (Serve one tomato per person if serving another vegetable, otherwise two each.)

SCRAMBLED EGGS

Plain and simple, or deluxe with additions, scrambled eggs are a reliable standby for quick suppers or breakfast.

4 to 6	**eggs**	**4 to 6**
2 tbsp	**milk per egg**	**25 mL**
¼ tsp	**salt**	**1 mL**
dash	**pepper**	**dash**
1 tbsp	**butter**	**15 mL**

1 In bowl, whisk eggs lightly with milk, salt and pepper.

2 In skillet (preferably non-stick) over medium heat, melt butter. Pour in egg mixture. Stir gently and as it begins to set, lift cooked portions with spatula or spoon so uncooked egg can flow underneath. Cook until eggs are set but still moist, about 3 minutes. Makes 2 servings.

VARIATIONS

SCRAMBLED EGGS DELUXE: Add any of the following (or a combination) to egg mixture in bowl:

1 cup (250 mL) shredded cheese; ½ cup (125 mL) chopped mushrooms, sliced cooked sausages, crumbled cooked bacon, chopped ham or green onions; ¼ cup (50 mL) chopped parsley or chives.

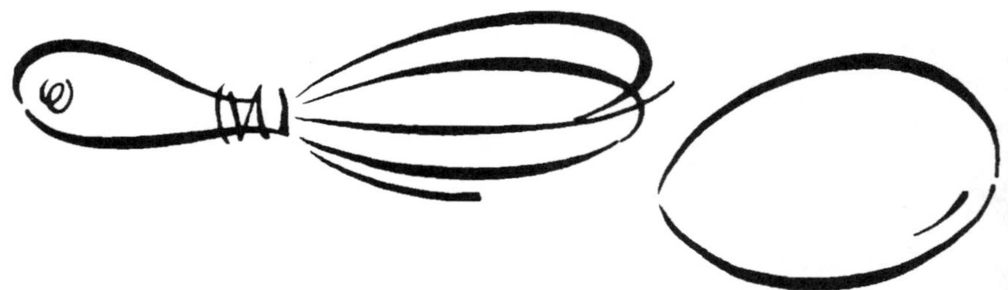

EASY EGGS BENEDICT

Poached Eggs

Fill wide shallow saucepan with water about 2 in/ 5 cm deep. Bring to boil; reduce to simmer. Break one egg into a small cup. With a spoon, swirl the simmering water into a small whirlpool (this will help form the egg into a rounded shape); slip egg into water. Repeat with remaining eggs. Poach in gently simmering water for 2 to 3 minutes (test by gently touching with finger; yolks should feel soft and slightly set). Remove with slotted

Try these for an indulgent brunch. Classic hollandaise sauce is difficult to make, but this version using the microwave and blender is a cinch.

2	**English muffins, split and toasted**	**2**
4	**thin slices cooked ham**	**4**
4	**poached eggs**	**4**
	Quick Hollandaise Sauce (see below)	

1 Have pan of water simmering and ready to poach the eggs. Then quickly make the hollandaise sauce; cover blender tightly so sauce stays warm.

2 Poach the eggs (see sidebar).

3 While eggs are poaching, toast the muffins.

4 Place muffins on 4 plates. Top with ham and poached egg. Spoon sauce over each. Makes 4 servings.

QUICK HOLLANDAISE SAUCE

3	**egg yolks**	**3**
1 tbsp	**lemon juice**	**15 mL**
pinch	**salt and white pepper**	**pinch**
⅔ cup	**butter (in glass measuring cup)**	**150 mL**

1 In blender, combine egg yolks, lemon juice, salt and pepper; blend about 5 seconds.

2 Heat butter in microwave on High until bubbling hot, about 1 ½ minutes.

3 With blender running, add hot butter in slow thin stream through the hole in the lid. The sauce will thicken as the butter is added; this takes only about 30 seconds.

FRITTATA

Frittata is an Italian egg dish, heartier than a French omelette and rather like a crustless quiche.

2 tbsp	**butter**	**25 mL**
½ cup	**chopped onions**	**125 mL**
½ cup	**chopped red or green pepper**	**125 mL**
½ cup	**sliced mushrooms**	**125 mL**
½ cup	**sliced small zucchini *or* cooked broccoli**	**125 mL**
6	**eggs**	**6**
½ tsp	**salt**	**2 mL**
dash	**pepper**	**dash**
1 cup	**shredded mozzarella cheese**	**250 mL**
2 tbsp	**chopped parsley**	**25 mL**
2 tbsp	**grated Parmesan cheese**	**25 mL**

1 Turn on oven broiler to preheat.

2 Meanwhile, in 10-inch (25 cm) skillet (preferably non-stick) over medium heat, melt butter. Add onions, peppers, mushrooms and zucchini; cook, stirring, about 3 minutes or until tender.

3 In bowl, whisk eggs with salt and pepper. Stir in mozzarella and parsley. Pour over vegetables in pan.

4 Cook until bottom of frittata sets, lifting edges with spatula to allow uncooked eggs to flow underneath. When bottom is golden brown but top is still moist, sprinkle with Parmesan.

5 Wrap skillet handle in foil if it's not ovenproof. Place skillet under broiler for 1 to 2 minutes or until frittata is set and lightly browned.

6 Slide frittata onto serving plate and cut in wedges. Makes 3 to 4 servings.

CHEESE STRATA

This is a popular make-ahead brunch dish; it's refrigerated overnight and baked in the morning.

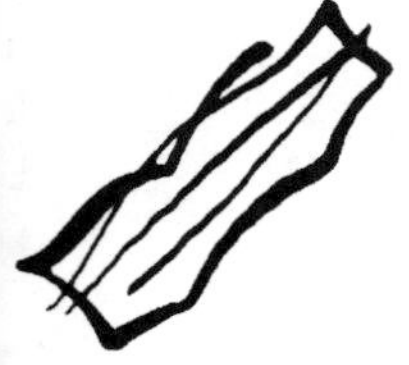

8	**slices firm-textured white bread**	**8**
1 ½ cups	**shredded Cheddar cheese**	**375 mL**
4	**slices ham *or* chopped crisp bacon**	**4**
4	**eggs**	**4**
2 cups	**milk**	**500 mL**
¼ tsp	**salt**	**1 mL**
dash	**pepper**	**dash**
dash	**Worcestershire sauce**	**dash**

1 Trim crusts from bread; butter bread lightly on both sides.

2 Arrange half of bread in buttered 9-inch (2.5 L) square pan. Sprinkle with half the cheese. Top with sliced ham or chopped bacon. Top with remaining bread and cheese.

3 Beat together eggs, milk, salt and Worcestershire sauce. Pour over bread. Cover and refrigerate overnight.

4 Preheat oven to 350°F (180°C). Bake uncovered for 45 minutes or until set in centre, puffed and golden brown.

5 Let stand for 5 minutes. Cut into squares. Makes about 4 servings.

FAST PASTA

These pasta dishes are delicious and really easy to make.

PASTA PRIMAVERA

You can make this two ways: with tomatoes (for a fresh tomato sauce) *or* with cream (for a creamy sauce).

½ lb	**spaghetti, fettucine or other pasta**	**250 g**
2 tbsp	**olive oil**	**25 mL**
¼ cup	**chopped onion**	**50 mL**
1	**clove garlic, minced**	**1**
½ cup	**each: chopped red or green pepper, sliced zucchini, small broccoli florets, sliced mushrooms**	**125 mL**
2	**ripe tomatoes, chopped *or* ½ cup (125 mL) whipped cream**	**2**
	Salt and pepper	
	Grated Parmesan cheese	

1. In a large pot of boiling salted water, cook pasta until tender but firm.
2. Meanwhile, in a large skillet, heat olive oil. Add onion, garlic, pepper, zucchini, broccoli, and mushrooms. Cover and cook until nearly tender, about 2 minutes.
3. For *Tomato Primavera,* add tomatoes, or for *Creamy Primavera,* add whipping cream.
4. Cook, stirring, about 2 minutes. Season with salt and pepper to taste. Toss with drained pasta. Top with Parmesan. Makes about 2 servings.

FETTUCINE ALFREDO

½ lb	fresh or dried fettucine	250 g
2 tbsp	butter	25 mL
¾ cup	whipping cream	175 mL
¾ cup	freshly grated Parmesan cheese	175 mL
	Salt and pepper	
	Chopped parsley	

1 In a large pot of boiling salted water, cook fettucine until tender but firm, about 3 minutes for pre-packaged fresh pasta or 6 minutes for dried.

2 Drain in colander; return to pot over medium heat. Add butter and toss.

3 Add cream and Parmesan. Stir until noodles are coated, about 2 minutes.

4 Add salt and pepper to taste. Serve immediately, sprinkled with chopped parsley and more Parmesan, if desired. Makes 2 to 3 servings.

RAVIOLI OR TORTELLINI CASSEROLE

See page 55 for recipe for Spaghetti Sauce.

¾ lb	Fresh or frozen ravioli or tortellini	375 g
1 ½ cups	spaghetti sauce (homemade or purchased)	375 mL
1 cup	shredded mozzarella cheese	250 mL
¼ cup	grated Parmesan cheese	50 mL

1 In pot of boiling salted water, cook pasta until tender but still firm, about 6 to 10 minutes. Drain well.

2 In 6-cup (1.5 L) casserole, combine pasta with spaghetti sauce. Sprinkle with mozzarella and Parmesan.

3 Bake in 350°F (180°C) oven for about 20 minutes or until bubbling hot. (Or microwave on High about 3 minutes.) Makes about 3 servings.

EASY MACARONI & CHEESE

Make a salad and a speedy microwave cheese sauce while the macaroni is cooking, and supper is ready.

1 cup	**uncooked macaroni**	**250 mL**
½ cup	**shredded Cheddar cheese (for topping)**	**125 mL**

Microwave Cheese Sauce:

2 tbsp	**butter**	**25 mL**
2 tbsp	**all-purpose flour**	**25 mL**
1 cup	**milk**	**250 mL**
¼ tsp	**salt**	**1 mL**
pinch	**pepper**	**pinch**
1 ½ cups	**shredded Cheddar cheese**	**375 mL**

1 In pot of boiling salted water, cook macaroni until tender, about 12 minutes.

2 MICROWAVE CHEESE SAUCE: In 4-cup (1 L) glass measuring cup or bowl, melt butter (about 20 seconds on High). Stir in flour, milk, salt and pepper. Microwave on High for 2 minutes; stir with whisk. Microwave on High for 2 minutes longer; stir with whisk. Stir in cheese until melted. Taste and add a little more salt and pepper if needed.

3 Drain macaroni well. Combine with hot sauce. Turn into microwavable baking dish. Sprinkle with shredded Cheddar. Microwave on High for 1 minute or until cheese is melted. Makes 2 to 3 servings.

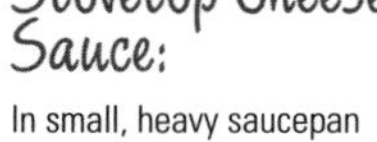

In small, heavy saucepan over medium heat, melt butter. Stir in flour until smooth. Gradually add milk, stirring with a wire whisk. Stirring constantly, bring to boil and boil gently for about 2 minutes until thickened and smooth. Add salt and pepper. Stir in cheese just until melted; remove from heat.

SPAGHETTI SAUCE

A good and easy all-purpose tomato sauce for spaghetti or any kind of pasta. Make it with meat or meatless.

1 tbsp	**olive oil**	**15 mL**
½ lb	**lean ground beef (optional)**	**250 g**
1	**small onion, finely chopped**	**1**
1	**clove garlic, minced**	**1**
½ tsp	**salt**	**2 mL**
¼ tsp	**pepper**	**1 mL**
½ tsp	**each: dried oregano and basil**	**2 mL**
2 tbsp	**tomato paste**	**25 mL**
1½ cups	**beef stock *or* water**	**375 mL**
1	**can (28 oz/796 mL) tomatoes**	**1**

1 In large heavy saucepan over medium heat, heat oil. Add ground beef (if using), onions and garlic. Cook, stirring until meat loses its pinkness and onion is soft, about 10 minutes.

2 Add salt, pepper, herbs, tomato paste and beef stock.

3 If tomatoes are whole, blend (with their juice) in food processor or blender until nearly smooth (or crush with potato masher). Add tomatoes to saucepan.

4 Simmer uncovered about 40 minutes or to desired thickness, stirring often. Season to taste with salt and pepper. Makes about 3 cups (750 mL).

EASY LASAGNA

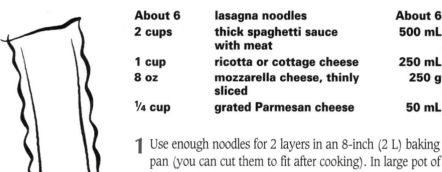

Most lasagna recipes are big-family or party size; this one is simpler to prepare for singles or couples. It makes about 4 servings, and leftovers reheat well in microwave. For the spaghetti sauce, use a thick bottled brand or the recipe on page 55.

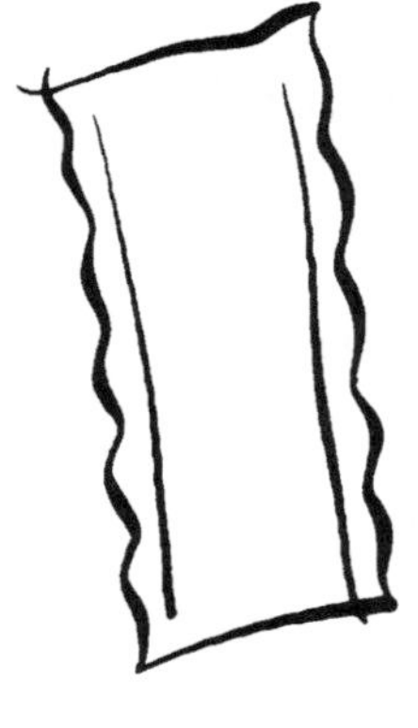

About 6	**lasagna noodles**	**About 6**
2 cups	**thick spaghetti sauce with meat**	**500 mL**
1 cup	**ricotta or cottage cheese**	**250 mL**
8 oz	**mozzarella cheese, thinly sliced**	**250 g**
¼ cup	**grated Parmesan cheese**	**50 mL**

1 Use enough noodles for 2 layers in an 8-inch (2 L) baking pan (you can cut them to fit after cooking). In large pot of boiling salted water, cook noodles until tender but firm, about 12 minutes; drain and rinse in cold water.

2 Meanwhile, preheat oven to 350°F (180°C).

3 Spread thin layer of sauce in bottom of baking pan. Top with half of noodles in single layer. Spread half of sauce over noodles; dot with half of ricotta; top with half of mozzarella and Parmesan. Repeat layers.

4 Bake uncovered for 30 minutes or until bubbling. Let stand 10 minutes before cutting into squares. Makes about 4 servings.

RICE PILAF

An easy way to dress up rice, pilaf is great with many meat dishes, especially lamb or chicken.

2 tbsp	**butter**	**25 mL**
¼ cup	**finely chopped onion**	**50 mL**
2 tbsp	**finely chopped celery**	**25 mL**
¾ cup	**long grain rice**	**175 mL**
1 ½ cups	**chicken stock**	**375 mL**
1 tbsp	**chopped parsley**	**15 mL**
	Salt and pepper	

1. In large heavy saucepan over medium-high heat, melt butter. Add onion and celery; cook until softened but not browned, about 2 minutes.
2. Add rice and cook, stirring often, until slightly golden, about 2 minutes.
3. Stir in stock; bring to boil. Reduce heat, cover and simmer for about 20 minutes or until rice is tender and all liquid is absorbed.
4. Stir in parsley, and salt and pepper to taste. Makes 3 to 4 servings.

BARLEY-MUSHROOM CASSEROLE

Grains are great for inexpensive, nutritious vegetarian dishes or as interesting alternatives to potatoes or rice. Barley has a pleasant chewy texture and mild flavour.

2 tbsp	**butter**	**25 mL**
¾ cup	**pearl barley**	**175 mL**
¼ cup	**chopped onions**	**50 mL**
¼ cup	**chopped celery**	**50 mL**
1 cup	**coarsely chopped mushrooms**	**250 mL**
2½ cups	**chicken or vegetable stock**	**625 mL**
¼ cup	**slivered almonds**	**50 mL**
2 tbsp	**chopped parsley**	**25 mL**
	Salt and pepper	

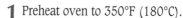

1 Preheat oven to 350°F (180°C).

2 In skillet over medium-high heat, melt butter. Add barley, onions, celery and mushrooms; cook, stirring until vegetables are softened and barley is lightly coloured, about 5 minutes.

3 Add stock; bring to boil.

4 Transfer mixture to 6 cup (1.5 L) casserole dish. Cover and bake for about 1 hour or until barley is tender and liquid is absorbed. Stir twice during last 30 minutes and add a little water if mixture becomes too dry. Add salt and pepper to taste.

5 Meanwhile, toast almonds in the oven (spread in shallow pan and bake until lightly browned, about 5 to 10 minutes).

6 Just before serving, stir in almonds and parsley. Makes about 4 servings.

QUICK CHILI

Serve in bowls with thick slices of toasted egg bread or wholewheat toast. Or cook chili until thicker and spoon it into taco shells or pitas.

1 lb	**ground beef**	**500 g**
1	**medium onion, chopped**	**1**
1	**clove garlic, minced**	**1**
2 tsp	**chili powder**	**10 mL**
½ tsp	**ground cumin**	**2 mL**
dash	**black and cayenne pepper**	**dash**
1	**can (15 oz/426 mL) tomato sauce**	**1**
1	**can (14 oz/398 mL) red kidney beans**	**1**

1 In large skillet (non-stick or lightly greased) over medium heat, cook ground beef until no pink colour remains, breaking it up well with spoon or fork. Drain off fat.

2 Add onions and garlic; cook until softened, about 3 minutes. Add spices; cook about 1 minute.

3 Add tomato sauce and kidney beans. Cover and simmer for 15 minutes, stirring occasionally. Uncover and simmer to desired thickness, 15 to 30 minutes. Season to taste with salt and pepper. Makes about 4 servings.

JAMAICAN RICE AND PEAS

Rice and peas are a common accompaniment to spicy meat and fish dishes, including Jerk Chicken.

See page 75 for Jerk Chicken recipe.

½ cup	**small red dried peas**	**125 mL**
1½ cups	**boiling salted water**	**375 mL**
½ cup	**canned coconut milk**	**125 mL**
1 cup	**rice**	**250 mL**
1	**small onion, chopped**	**1**
¼ tsp	**dried thyme**	**1 mL**
½ tsp	**salt**	**2 mL**
pinch	**black pepper**	**pinch**

1 In large, heavy saucepan, boil peas in water until tender, about 1 hour.

2 Drain and measure cooking liquid; add coconut milk plus enough water to make 2 cups (500 mL) of liquid. Add the liquid to peas in saucepan.

3 Add rice, onion, thyme, salt and pepper.

4 Cover and simmer until liquid is absorbed and rice is tender, about 30 minutes. Add more salt and pepper to taste if needed. Makes about 4 servings.

Every Caribbean island has its own version of rice and peas (which happen to be a good combination of complete protein). Jamaicans usually use small red peas (sometimes called cow peas); you can substitute any other kind in this recipe. Caribbean ingredients are available in many supermarkets as well as West Indian shops.

EASY OVEN STEW

With this recipe, you don't have to brown the meat first (so it's much easier and lower in fat, too), but it still makes a rich-tasting stew or thick, chunky soup. Serve it in big soup bowls with lots of crusty bread.

Chunky Beef Vegetable Soup

For Chunky Beef Vegetable Soup, add a little more water, and extra vegetables such as green peas, beans or diced turnip.

1 ½ lbs	**stewing beef**	**750 g**
1	**large onion, chopped**	**1**
1	**clove garlic, minced**	**1**
2 tbsp	**all-purpose flour**	**25 mL**
1 tsp	**salt**	**5 mL**
¼ tsp	**pepper**	**1 mL**
¼ tsp	**dried thyme**	**1 mL**
1	**can (10 oz/284 mL) beef broth**	**1**
1	**can (7 ½ oz/213 mL) tomato sauce**	**1**
1 cup	**water**	**250 mL**
1	**small bay leaf**	**1**
2	**carrots, sliced**	**2**
2	**potatoes, diced**	**2**

1. Preheat oven to 350°F (180°C).
2. Trim beef and cut in small chunks. Place in large, heavy casserole or ovenproof pot with lid.
3. Add onion, garlic, flour, salt, pepper and thyme; mix well. Stir in beef broth, tomato sauce and water. Add bay leaf and carrots.
4. Cover and bake for 2 hours or until meat is very tender, stirring occasionally; add the potatoes for the last 30 minutes of cooking. Add a little more water if needed.
5. Remove bay leaf. Taste and add salt or pepper if needed. Makes about 4 servings. (Also very good reheated.)

RED-TOP MEATLOAF

This is really easy and delicious. For a complete oven meal, make Baked Potatoes and Baked Apples at the same time.

See page 41 for Baked Potatoes, see page 93 for Baked Apples.

1 ½ lbs	**ground beef**	**750 g**
½ cup	**quick-cooking rolled oats (not instant)**	**125 mL**
¾ cup	**finely chopped onion**	**175 mL**
½ cup	**milk**	**125 mL**
1	**egg**	**1**
1 tbsp	**Worcestershire sauce**	**15 mL**
1 tsp	**salt**	**5 mL**
½ tsp	**pepper**	**2 mL**
¼ cup	**ketchup, chili sauce or salsa**	**50 mL**

1. Preheat oven to 350°F (180°C).
2. In large bowl, combine all ingredients except ketchup, mixing thoroughly with spoon or hands.
3. Pack into 8 ½ x 4 ½ inch (1.5 L) loaf pan (non-stick or lightly greased). Spread ketchup over top.
4. Bake for 1 hour. Drain off any fat or liquid in pan; with metal spatula, transfer meatloaf to platter. Cut in slices. Makes 4 to 6 servings.

BEEF NOODLE SKILLET DINNER

Transform ordinary hamburger into an easy one-dish supper that tastes great and is good for you, too (this recipe contains all four food groups). You could substitute any kind of pasta (such as rotini) for the noodles, or use Italian-seasoned tomato sauce or stewed tomatoes instead of spaghetti sauce. Serve with a crisp green salad.

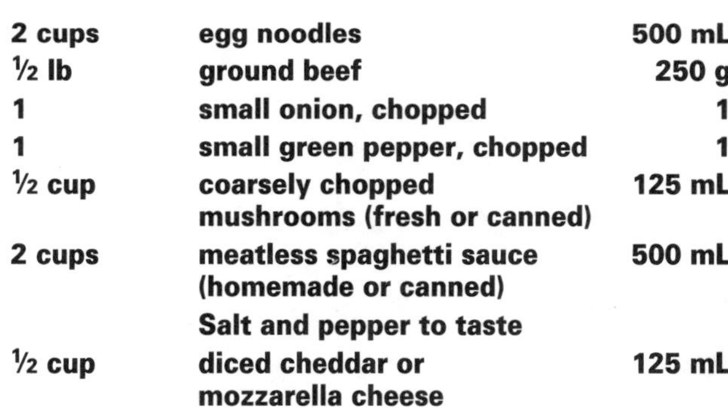

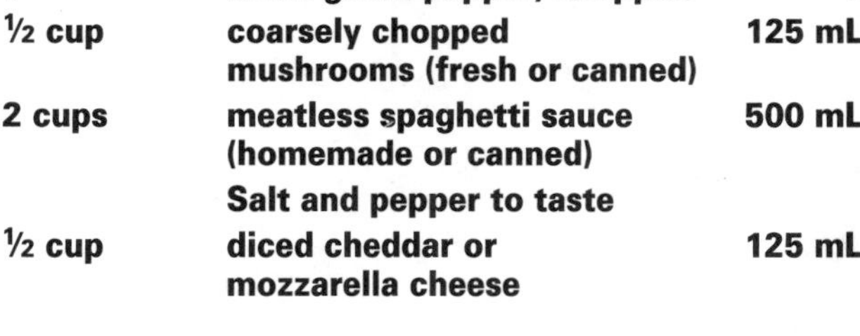

2 cups	**egg noodles**	**500 mL**
½ lb	**ground beef**	**250 g**
1	**small onion, chopped**	**1**
1	**small green pepper, chopped**	**1**
½ cup	**coarsely chopped mushrooms (fresh or canned)**	**125 mL**
2 cups	**meatless spaghetti sauce (homemade or canned)**	**500 mL**
	Salt and pepper to taste	
½ cup	**diced cheddar or mozzarella cheese**	**125 mL**

1 Cook noodles in large pot of boiling, salted water until tender but still firm (about 6 minutes). Drain and set aside.

2 Meanwhile, in large skillet (preferably non-stick) over medium heat, cook ground beef until no pink colour remains; stir often to break up meat as it cooks. Drain off fat.

3 Add onion, green pepper and mushrooms. Cook, stirring often, until softened, about 2 minutes.

4 Stir in sauce. Season with salt and pepper if needed. Stir in cheese.

5 Add noodles to skillet. Stir to combine, then cover for 1 to 2 minutes or until hot. Makes about 3 servings.

Prepare skillet dinner, omitting diced cheese. Pour mixture into 6-cup (1.5 L) casserole dish. Sprinkle top with **½ cup (125 mL) shredded cheese.** (May be refrigerated at this point to bake later.) Cover and bake in 350°F (180°C) oven for about 20 minutes (30 to 40 minutes if refrigerated) or until bubbling hot.

More pork recipes! Stir-Fried Pork & Vegetables, page 68, Pork Schnitzel, page 70, Pork Parmigiana, page 70.

SWEET & SOUR PORK CHOPS WITH LEMON

A citrus-flavoured sauce dresses up pork chops for a quick supper. Serve with rice and green peas.

4	**pork chops**	**4**
1 tbsp	**vegetable oil**	**15 mL**
	Salt and pepper	
4	**thin slices onion**	**4**
8	**thin slices unpeeled lemon**	**8**
¼ cup	**brown sugar**	**50 mL**
2 tsp	**cornstarch**	**10 mL**
¼ cup	**orange juice**	**50 mL**
¼ cup	**white vinegar**	**50 mL**
1 tbsp	**soy sauce**	**15 mL**

1. Trim most of fat from edge of chops.
2. In large skillet (preferably non-stick) over medium heat, heat oil. Add chops and cook until lightly browned, about 2 minutes on each side. Sprinkle lightly with salt and pepper.
3. Top each chop with slice of onion and two slices of lemon.
4. In small bowl, mix together brown sugar and cornstarch; stir in orange juice, vinegar and soy sauce until smooth; pour over chops.
5. Cover and simmer about 10 minutes, spooning sauce over chops occasionally. Makes 4 servings.

VARIATION

SWEET & SOUR PORK CHOPS WITH PINEAPPLE: Use pineapple juice instead of orange juice; omit onion and lemon slices and add a few canned pineapple tidbits to sauce.

Sweet & Sour Chicken (Lemon or Pineapple)

Use chicken breasts (bone-in or boneless) instead of pork chops. For bone-in, increase cooking time to about 20 minutes.

BARBECUED SPARERIBS

Bake these zesty ribs in the oven or grill them on the barbecue. The secret to tender, juicy ribs is to simmer them first, then bake or barbecue with sauce.

2 ½ lbs	**pork spareribs**	**1.25 kg**
Spicy Barbecue Sauce:		
¾ cup	**ketchup**	**175 mL**
¾ cup	**hot salsa**	**175 mL**
¼ cup	**brown sugar**	**50 mL**
2 tbsp	**vinegar**	**25 mL**
1 tsp	**Worcestershire sauce**	**5 mL**

1 Cut spareribs into portions of 2 or 3 ribs each. In large saucepan, cover ribs with salted water; bring to gentle boil; cook, covered, for 45 minutes or until tender. Drain ribs and place in one layer in 13 x 9-inch (3.5 L) baking pan.

2 SPICY BARBECUE SAUCE: Combine all ingredients; pour over ribs. Marinate in refrigerator for about 2 hours.

3 TO OVEN BAKE: Bake in 400°F (200°C) oven for about 40 minutes, turning and basting occasionally, until ribs are a rich colour and well coated with sauce.
TO BARBECUE: Remove ribs from sauce; reserve sauce. Place ribs on grill over medium hot coals (or medium setting on gas barbecue). Cook for about 20 minutes, turning and brushing with reserved sauce occasionally, until well coated with sauce and browned. Makes about 4 servings.

See page 19 for Honey-Garlic Sauce recipe.

VARIATION

HONEY GARLIC RIBS: Use Honey-Garlic Sauce instead of Spicy Barbecue Sauce.

BROILED LAMB CHOPS

One of the simplest and best ways to cook lamb chops, this uses a garlic-herb marinade for extra flavour. For tender, juicy chops be sure not to overcook.

6 to 8	**lamb loin chops (fresh or thawed)**	**6 to 8**
¼ cup	**olive oil**	**50 mL**
1 tbsp	**red wine vinegar *or* lemon juice**	**15 mL**
1	**large clove garlic, crushed**	**1**
1 tsp	**each: dried rosemary and basil**	**5 mL**
¼ tsp	**pepper**	**1 mL**

1 Place chops in single layer in glass dish. Combine remaining ingredients. Pour over chops, turning to coat both sides. Marinate in refrigerator for 1 to 2 hours.

2 Preheat oven broiler. Place chops on broiler rack.

3 Broil about 4 inches (10 cm) below heat for about 4 minutes on each side, or until browned outside but pink in centre. Makes 2 to 3 servings.

SOUVLAKI

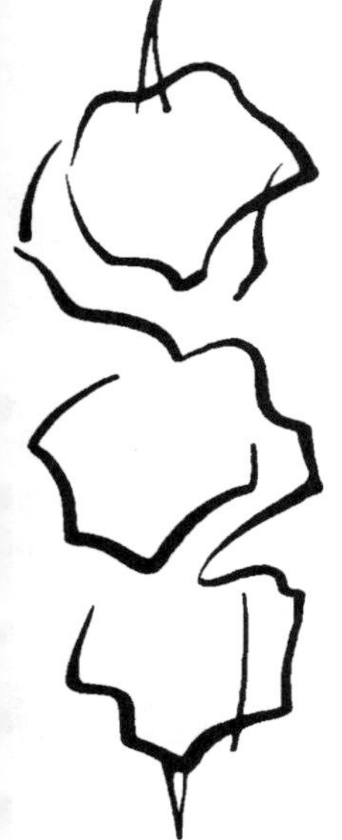

A Greek specialty, sizzling lamb kabobs are great with a dip of garlicky tzatziki. Souvlaki is often made with long strips of lamb threaded on skewers, but cubes of lamb are easier.

1 ½ lbs	**boneless lamb leg or shoulder**	**750 g**
⅓ cup	**olive oil**	**75 mL**
¼ cup	**lemon juice**	**50 mL**
1 tbsp	**red wine vinegar**	**15 mL**
2	**cloves garlic, minced**	**2**
1 tsp	**each: dried oregano and rosemary**	**5 mL**
¼ tsp	**pepper**	**1 mL**
	About 12 short skewers (see note)	

1 Cut lamb into ¾-inch (2 cm) cubes.

2 In bowl, combine oil, lemon juice, vinegar, garlic, herbs and pepper. Add lamb cubes, turning to coat. Marinate in refrigerator for 2 to 4 hours, stirring occasionally.

3 Remove lamb from marinade; reserve marinade. Thread lamb onto skewers (3 or 4 cubes fairly close together on each).

4 Preheat oven broiler or barbecue (medium-hot coals or medium-hot setting on gas). Broil or grill meat for about 8 minutes, turning occasionally and brushing with marinade, until browned outside but pink inside.

5 Serve with Tzatziki Dip. Makes about 6 appetizer servings. (For a main course, serve with Rice Pilaf and Greek Salad.)

NOTE: Small metal skewers are fine, but wooden skewers look nicer for serving (soak them in water for 30 minutes before threading).

Tzatziki Dip

Tzatziki is a thick yogurt sauce; this is a simplified version: Put **1 cup (250 mL)** coarsely grated cucumber (peeled, seedless) into a sieve; squeeze out excess moisture. Combine cucumber with **½ cup (125 mL)** each plain yogurt and light sour cream, **2 minced cloves garlic, 1 tsp (5 mL) dried dillweed** and **salt** and **pepper** to taste. Refrigerate 1 hour to blend flavours.

STIR-FRIED CHICKEN & VEGETABLES

Stir-frying is a fast and easy way to cook meats and vegetables for busy-day suppers. This is a good basic stir-fry to vary as you wish.

2 tbsp	**vegetable oil**	**30 mL**
½ lb	**boneless chicken breast, cut in strips**	**250 g**
1	**onion, coarsely chopped**	**1**
1	**clove garlic, minced**	**1**
1 tsp	**minced fresh ginger (optional)**	**5 mL**
½ cup	**diagonally sliced celery**	**125 mL**
½ cup	**sliced red or green pepper**	**125 mL**
½ cup	**broccoli florets**	**125 mL**
½ cup	**sliced zucchini**	**125 mL**
½ cup	**chicken stock**	**125 mL**
2 tbsp	**soy sauce**	**25 mL**
2 tsp	**cornstarch**	**10 mL**
	Salt and pepper	

1. In wok or large skillet over medium-high heat, heat 1 tbsp (15 mL) oil. Add chicken; stir-fry (stirring quickly and constantly) for about 3 minutes or until chicken is just cooked through. Remove chicken to a bowl; set aside.
2. Add remaining oil to pan; add onion, garlic, ginger (if using) and vegetables; stir-fry about 1 minute.
3. Add chicken stock; cover and let steam for about 2 minutes or until vegetables are tender-crisp.
4. Return chicken to pan. Mix together soy sauce and cornstarch; stir into pan. Cook, stirring, until thickened, about 1 minute. Season with salt and pepper to taste. Makes 2 servings.

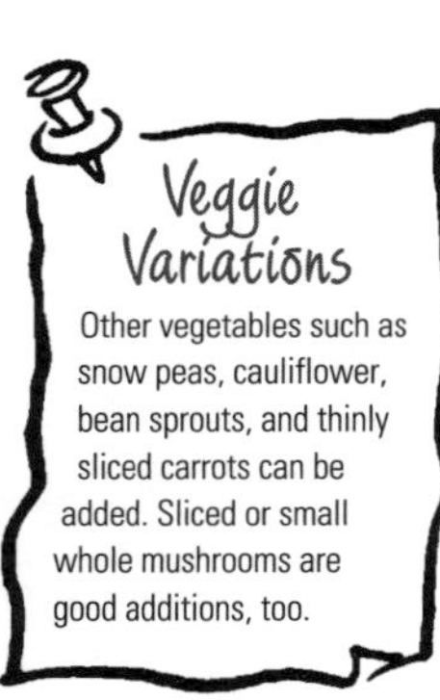

Veggie Variations

Other vegetables such as snow peas, cauliflower, bean sprouts, and thinly sliced carrots can be added. Sliced or small whole mushrooms are good additions, too.

Stir-fried Turkey, Pork or Beef & Vegetables

Instead of chicken, use boneless turkey, lean pork or beef. (Less tender cuts of beef are best cut in thin slices across the grain rather than cubes.)

CHICKEN CACCIATORE

Serve over pasta such as spaghettini or flat noodles.

2 lbs	**chicken pieces**	**1 kg**
	Flour, salt and pepper	
2 tbsp	**olive oil**	**25 mL**
1	**medium onion, chopped**	**1**
2	**cloves garlic, minced**	**2**
1	**small green pepper, chopped or cut in strips**	**1**
½ cup	**chopped celery**	**125 mL**
1 cup	**sliced mushrooms**	**250 mL**
½ tsp	**each: dried basil and oregano**	**2 mL**
1	**can (28 oz/796 mL) tomatoes (whole or diced)**	**1**
	Salt and pepper	

1 Dust chicken with flour and sprinkle lightly with salt and pepper.

2 In large skillet (preferably non-stick) over medium heat, heat oil. Brown chicken pieces lightly on all sides. Drain off most of fat.

3 Add onion, garlic, pepper, celery and mushrooms. Cook, stirring occasionally, for about 5 minutes until softened.

4 Add herbs and tomatoes (if whole, crush them as you add them). Cover and simmer for about 30 minutes or until chicken is very tender. (If sauce is too thin, remove cover and simmer until sauce thickens.) Season to taste with salt and pepper. Makes about 4 servings.

Chicken and Sausage Cacciatore

Brown **3 Italian sausages** with the chicken, then cut each sausage into 4 pieces.

CHICKEN SCHNITZEL

Boneless meats cook very quickly; a crispy crumb coating keeps them moist and tender.

4	**boneless skinless chicken breasts (8 if very small)**	**4**
1	**egg, lightly beaten**	**1**
¾ cup	**fine dry breadcrumbs**	**175 mL**
	Salt and pepper	
2 tbsp	**vegetable oil**	**25 mL**
	Lemon wedges	

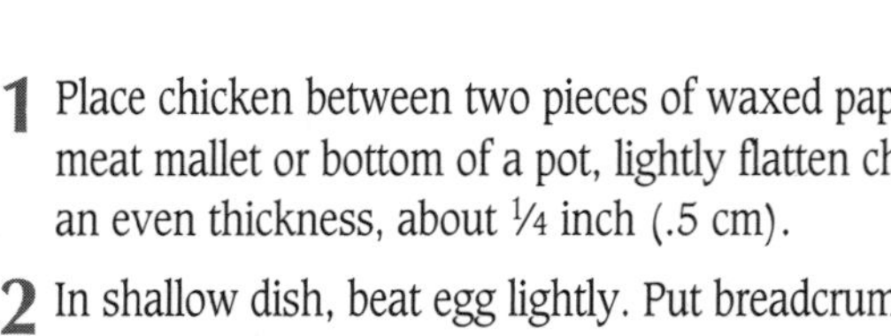

1 Place chicken between two pieces of waxed paper; with meat mallet or bottom of a pot, lightly flatten chicken to an even thickness, about ¼ inch (.5 cm).

2 In shallow dish, beat egg lightly. Put breadcrumbs in another dish. Dip chicken in egg, then into breadcrumbs to coat evenly. Sprinkle lightly on both sides with salt and pepper.

3 In large skillet (preferably non-stick) over medium heat, heat oil. Add chicken and cook until golden brown and cooked through, about 4 minutes on each side. Makes 4 servings.

VARIATIONS

CHICKEN PARMIGIANA: Pour 1 cup (250 mL) tomato sauce around browned chicken. Top each piece with slice of mozzarella cheese; sprinkle with ¼ cup (50 mL) grated Parmesan. Cover and simmer until cheese is melted, about 2 minutes.

TURKEY, PORK OR VEAL SCHNITZEL (OR PARMIGIANA): Use boneless turkey breast, pork or veal cutlets instead of chicken.

CHICKEN OR TURKEY BURGERS

Ground chicken or turkey makes great low-fat burgers and can also be used instead of ground beef in meatloaf or other recipes.

1 lb	**ground chicken or turkey**	**500 g**
¼ cup	**finely chopped onion**	**50 mL**
1	**clove garlic, minced**	**1**
½ tsp	**salt *or* seasoned salt**	**2 mL**
¼ tsp	**pepper**	**1 mL**
	Thinly sliced or shredded cheese (optional)	
4	**toasted buns *or* warmed pitas**	**4**

Suggested Toppings

Salsa, crisp lettuce, sliced onion, tomatoes, crisp bacon, lightly cooked peppers or mushrooms.

1 In bowl, combine ground chicken or turkey, onion, garlic, salt and pepper; mix well with your hands. Shape into 4 patties about ½ inch (1 cm) thick.

2 In lightly greased skillet (preferably non-stick) over medium heat, cook burgers for about 3 minutes on each side, or until golden and just cooked through. (Burgers can also be barbecued or broiled.) Sprinkle with more salt and pepper to taste.

3 If desired, top burgers with cheese; continue cooking until cheese melts.

4 Serve in buns or pitas with choice of toppings. Makes 4 burgers.

ROAST CHICKEN

When you're needing some comfort food, nothing beats the aroma and flavour of an old-fashioned roast chicken. Try it—it's really easy!

1	**chicken (about 3½ lb/1.5 kg)**	**1**
2 tbsp	**melted butter**	**25 mL**
Stuffing:		
4	**slices slightly dry bread**	**4**
¼ cup	**butter**	**50 mL**
1	**small onion, chopped**	**1**
1	**stalk celery, chopped**	**1**
2 tsp	**dried herbs (poultry seasoning, sage or savory)**	**10 mL**
¼ tsp	**salt**	**1 mL**
dash	**pepper**	**dash**

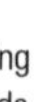

Unstuffed Chicken

Traditional bread stuffing is easy to make and adds great flavour, but if you don't want to make it, just sprinkle the inside of the chicken with salt, pepper and a teaspoonful of dried herbs (sage, savory, thyme or rosemary) and put an onion (cut in quarters) in the cavity. Reduce the roasting time by about 15 minutes.

1 Preheat oven to 350°F (180°C).

2 Rinse inside of chicken with cold water; dry chicken inside and out with paper towels.

3 STUFFING: Stack bread slices together; with bread knife, cut into small cubes (you should have about 4 cups/1L); place in large bowl. In glass measuring cup or bowl, combine butter, onion, celery, herbs, salt and pepper; microwave on High for about 1½ minutes or until softened. (Or cook in small saucepan on stove.) Add to bread and toss well. Taste and add more seasoning if needed.

4 Fill cavity of chicken with stuffing. Cover opening with an end slice of bread or fasten shut with a metal skewer.

5 Tie legs of chicken together tightly with string.

6 Place chicken, breast side up, in shallow roasting pan (a large rectangular cake pan is fine). Brush chicken with melted butter.

7 Cover chicken very loosely with foil, tucking it in at the sides but leaving ends open.

8 Roast for 1 ½ hours; remove foil and brush chicken with pan drippings. Roast *uncovered* for about 30 minutes longer until golden brown. (Don't overcook but check that the chicken is done; the thigh should feel soft when pressed, and the juices should be clear, not pink, when thigh is pricked with fork.) Makes about 4 servings.

CHICKEN GRAVY: Remove roasted chicken from pan; cover with foil to keep warm. Measure the **fat drippings** left in pan (you should have about **2 tbsp/25 mL**; if not, add some **butter**). Place pan over medium-high heat on stove. Stir **2 tbsp (25 mL) flour** into the fat; stir until bubbly, scraping up any brown bits on bottom of pan. Then stir in **1½ cups (375 mL) chicken broth**. Bring to boil, stirring constantly. Reduce heat and boil gently for 2 minutes until thickened and smooth. Taste and add salt and pepper if needed.

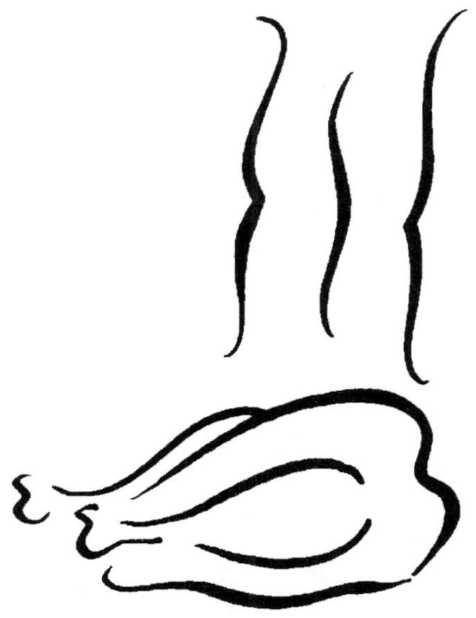

CHINESE ROASTED CHICKEN

Chicken roasted this way has a delicious Oriental flavour and dark brown skin. The main ingredient is hoisin sauce (available in most supermarkets).

2½ lb	**chicken halves or quarters**	**1.25 kg**
½ cup	**hoisin sauce**	**125 mL**
2 tbsp	**each: soy sauce, vinegar and ketchup**	**25 mL**
2 tsp	**minced garlic**	**10 mL**

1 Place chicken in foil-lined baking pan.

2 Combine remaining ingredients.

3 Brush half of the sauce all over chicken pieces; reserve remaining sauce.

4 Refrigerate for about 2 hours to flavour the chicken.

5 Roast in 375°F (190°C) oven for 45 to 60 minutes, brushing occasionally with reserved sauce, until chicken is cooked through and skin is well browned. (If it starts to brown too much, cover loosely with foil.) Makes about 4 servings.

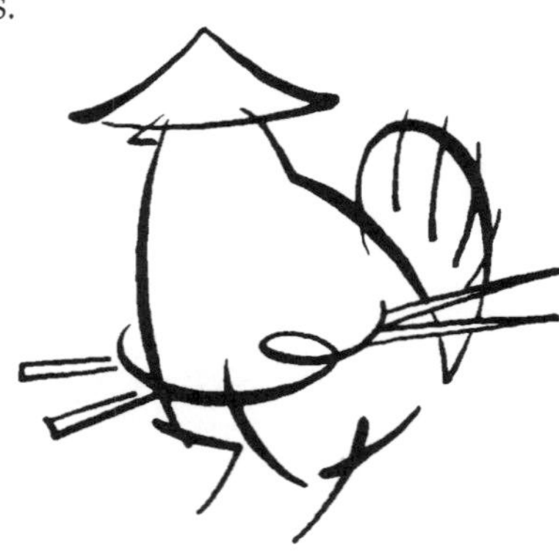

JERK CHICKEN

Hot-and-spicy grilled chicken is terrific party food (double the recipe for a larger crowd). Serve with Jamaican Rice and Peas.

See recipe for Jamaican Rice and Peas on page 60.

2 lbs	**chicken pieces (legs, thighs, breasts)**	**1 kg**
Marinade:		
2 tsp	**each: ground allspice and thyme**	**10 mL**
½ tsp	**each: black and cayenne pepper**	**2 mL**
¼ tsp	**each: cinnamon and nutmeg**	**1 mL**
2 tsp	**each: salt and sugar**	**10 mL**
¼ cup	**vegetable oil**	**50 mL**
½ cup	**white vinegar**	**125 mL**
¼ cup	**lime juice**	**50 mL**
1	**small onion, finely chopped**	**1**
3	**cloves garlic, minced**	**3**

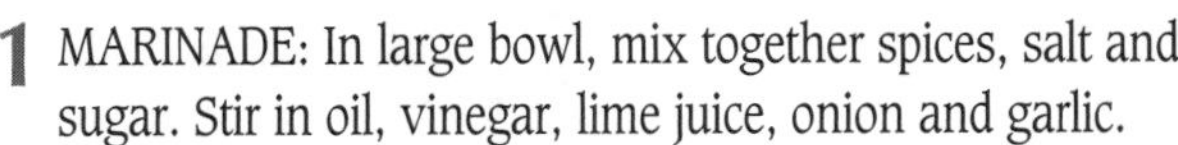

1 MARINADE: In large bowl, mix together spices, salt and sugar. Stir in oil, vinegar, lime juice, onion and garlic.

2 Add chicken, turning to coat with marinade. Cover and refrigerate for 2 to 4 hours, stirring occasionally.

3 Grill over medium hot coals or at medium setting on gas barbecue, turning chicken occasionally and basting often with marinade, for about 30 minutes or until cooked through. Makes 4 to 6 servings.

FAST FISH

Microwaved or oven-baked fish fillets are fast and delicious. You can create different flavours by adding any of the toppings suggested here, or make up your own favourites.

1 lb	**fish fillets, fresh or thawed**	**500 g**
1 tbsp	**lemon juice**	**15 mL**
	Salt and pepper	

In shallow round microwavable dish, arrange fillets in spoke pattern, with thicker parts at edges of dish. Sprinkle with lemon juice, and a little salt and pepper. Scatter topping ingredients over fish. Cover with waxed paper. Microwave on High for 5 to 7 minutes or until fish is opaque.

LEMON ALMOND TOPPING

½	**lemon, thinly sliced**	**½**
2 tbsp	**chopped parsley**	**25 mL**
½ cup	**toasted almonds (sprinkle on fish after cooking, just before serving)**	**125 mL**

To Oven Bake

In baking dish, arrange fish fillets in single layer. Sprinkle with lemon juice, and a little salt and pepper. Scatter topping ingredients over fish. Cover and bake at 425°F (220°C) for about 15 minutes or until fish flakes easily with a fork.

TOMATO PARMESAN TOPPING

½ cup	**chopped canned tomatoes**	**125 mL**
2 tbsp	**chopped onion**	**25 mL**
2 tbsp	**chopped green pepper**	**25 mL**
½ tsp	**dried oregano**	**2 mL**
¼ cup	**grated Parmesan cheese**	**50 mL**

MUSHROOM HERB TOPPING

1 cup	**sliced mushrooms**	**250 mL**
¼ cup	**chopped green onions**	**50 mL**
1 tsp	**dried basil**	**5 mL**

OVEN-FRIED FISH FILLETS

Crispy outside and moist inside, these are low-fat and easy to bake with Oven-Baked French Fries.

See page 42 for Oven-Baked French Fries recipe.

1 lb	**fish fillets (fresh or frozen)**	**500 g**
1 cup	**finely crushed potato chips *or* cornflake crumbs**	**250 mL**
1	**egg**	**1**
1 tbsp	**melted butter *or* vegetable oil**	**15 mL**
	Lemon wedges	

1. If fish is frozen, thaw just enough to separate fillets. To crush chips, place in plastic bag and crush with rolling pin, then measure. Place in shallow bowl.
2. Preheat oven to 450°F (230°C). Grease a baking sheet.
3. In shallow bowl, beat egg lightly. Dip fish into egg, then into crumbs, pressing crumbs to stick. Place on baking sheet. Drizzle with butter or oil.
4. Bake for 7 to 10 minutes or until fish flakes easily when tested with a fork. Don't overcook.
5. Sprinkle with salt and pepper to taste. Serve with lemon wedges. Makes about 4 servings.

TERIYAKI SALMON STEAKS

Oriental seasoning is great with salmon. These steaks can be broiled or barbecued; serve with rice and crisp-cooked broccoli, snow peas or stir-fried Chinese vegetables.

4	**salmon steaks**	**4**
½ cup	**light soy sauce**	**125 mL**
2 tbsp	**lemon juice *or* rice wine vinegar**	**25 mL**
2 tbsp	**sugar**	**25 mL**
1	**clove garlic, minced**	**1**
2 tsp	**minced fresh ginger root**	**10 mL**
¼ tsp	**pepper**	**1 mL**

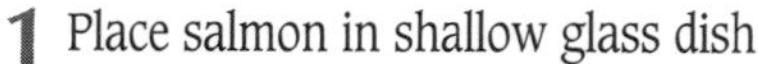

1. Place salmon in shallow glass dish.
2. Combine remaining ingredients and pour over salmon. Marinate for 2 hours in refrigerator.
3. Remove salmon from marinade; reserve marinade. **TO BROIL IN OVEN:** Place salmon on greased broiler pan about 4 inches (10 cm) under preheated broiler. **TO BARBECUE:** Place on rack over medium-hot coals or in gas barbecue at medium-high setting.
4. Broil or barbecue salmon for 3 to 4 minutes on each side, or just until it flakes easily with a fork but is still moist. Don't overcook. Turn only once; brush several times with marinade. Makes 4 servings.

BEST BRAN MUFFINS

Snack on great-tasting, good-for-you muffins fresh from the oven, or keep them handy for lunchboxes. This recipe has easy variations.

1	**egg**	**1**
1 cup	**milk**	**250 mL**
½ cup	**vegetable oil**	**125 mL**
¼ cup	**honey *or* 2 tbsp (25 mL) molasses**	**50 mL**
½ cup	**packed brown sugar**	**125 mL**
1 ½ cups	**natural wheat bran**	**375 mL**
1 cup	**wholewheat flour**	**250 mL**
1 tsp	**baking powder**	**5 mL**
1 tsp	**baking soda**	**5 mL**
½ tsp	**salt**	**2 mL**
½ cup	**raisins**	**125 mL**

1 Preheat oven to 400°F (200°C).

2 Line medium muffin tin with paper liners (about 12).

3 In large mixing bowl, beat together egg, milk, oil, honey and sugar. Stir in bran.

4 In small bowl, mix together flour, baking powder, baking soda and salt.

5 Add all at once to egg mixture; stir just until blended. Stir in raisins; don't overmix.

6 Spoon batter into muffin tins, filling each almost to top. (For easy filling, use a ¼-cup or 50 mL measure.)

7 Bake for 18 to 20 minutes or until firm to touch.

8 Let cool 5 minutes in pan, then remove muffins to wire rack to cool. Makes about 12 muffins.

Oat Bran Muffins

Use oat bran instead of wheat bran.

Honey Yogurt Bran Muffins

Use honey rather than molasses;molasses; use plain yogurt instead of milk.

Blueberry or Cranberry Bran Muffins

Gently stir in fresh or frozen blueberries or cranberries instead of raisins.

BANANA BREAD

This is one of the easiest recipes for popular banana bread. Use overripe bananas for best flavour and moistness.

2	**eggs**	**2**
3/4 cup	**granulated sugar**	**175 mL**
1/2 cup	**vegetable oil**	**125 mL**
1 cup	**mashed overripe bananas (about 3 medium)**	**250 mL**
2 cups	**all-purpose flour**	**500 mL**
1 tsp	**baking powder**	**5 mL**
1 tsp	**baking soda**	**5 mL**
1/2 tsp	**salt**	**2 mL**

1. Preheat oven to 350°F (180°C).
2. Grease and flour 8½ x 4½-inch (1.5 L) loaf pan.
3. In mixing bowl, combine eggs, sugar, oil and bananas; beat with egg beater or electric mixer until thoroughly blended.
4. In small bowl, mix together flour, baking powder, baking soda and salt. Add to egg mixture; stir until combined.
5. Pour into prepared pan.
6. Bake for 55 to 60 minutes or until tester inserted in centre comes out clean.
7. Let cool in pan for 5 minutes, then loosen edges with knife, and turn bread out onto rack to cool completely.

Spiced Banana Coconut Bread

Add ½ cup (125 mL) dessicated coconut and ½ tsp (2 mL) each cinnamon, nutmeg and allspice to flour mixture.

Banana Muffins

Spoon batter into paper-lined muffin tins, filling almost to top. Bake for 20 minutes or until tester comes out clean. Makes about 12.

HOT BISCUITS

Delicious served warm and buttered for a snack or with dinner, basic tea biscuits are very quick and easy to make after a little practice. Then try the great cinnamon rolls.

2 cups	**all-purpose flour**	**500 mL**
1 tbsp	**granulated sugar**	**15 mL**
4 tsp	**baking powder**	**20 mL**
1 tsp	**salt**	**5 mL**
½ cup	**shortening**	**125 mL**
¾ cup	**milk**	**175 mL**

1 Preheat oven to 425°F (220°C).

2 In large bowl, combine flour, sugar, baking powder and salt; stir thoroughly to mix.

3 Cut in shortening with a pastry blender until mixture looks like coarse crumbs.

4 Add milk all at once, stirring quickly with a fork to make a soft, slightly sticky dough.

5 Turn out onto lightly floured surface. Gather into a ball and knead very lightly about 10 times.

6 Roll dough out to ¾-inch (2 cm) thickness. Cut into biscuits with 3-inch (8 cm) round cookie cutter. Place biscuits on ungreased baking sheet.

7 Bake for 10 to 12 minutes or until golden brown. Makes about 12 biscuits.

VARIATION

RAISIN OR CHEESE TEA BISCUITS: Add 1 cup (250 mL) raisins or shredded Cheddar cheese to the flour mixture after cutting in shortening.

Quick Cinnamon Rolls

Roll dough out to 10-inch (25 cm) square. Brush with **¼ cup (50 mL) melted butter.** Mix together **⅔ cup (150 mL) brown sugar, 1 tsp (5 mL) cinnamon** and **⅓ cup (75 mL) raisins;** sprinkle evenly over dough. Roll up dough; pinch long edge to seal. Cut into 9 slices. Place slices, cut side down, evenly spaced in greased 8-inch (2 L) cake pan. Bake in 425°F (220°C) oven for 15 to 20 minutes or until golden brown. Let stand in pan about 3 minutes, then turn out onto wire rack. Serve warm. Makes 9 rolls.

WHOLEWHEAT SODA BREAD

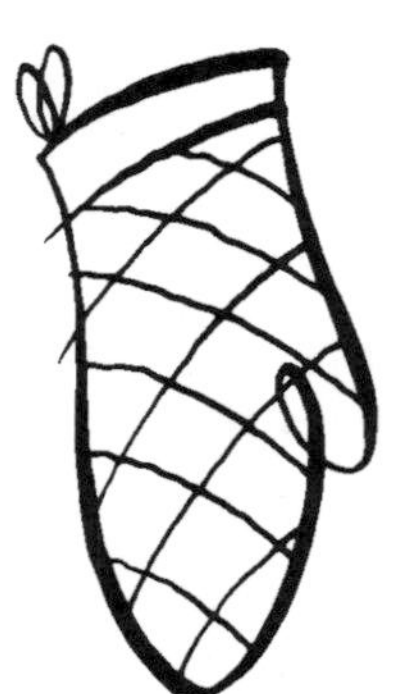

This recipe quickly makes two nice round loaves of a wholesome, old-fashioned bread that tastes and smells wonderful.

2 cups	**all-purpose flour**	**500 mL**
2 cups	**wholewheat flour**	**500 mL**
1/4 cup	**granulated sugar**	**50 mL**
1 tbsp	**baking powder**	**15 mL**
1 tsp	**baking soda**	**5 mL**
1 1/2 tsp	**salt**	**7 mL**
1/4 cup	**butter**	**50 mL**
1	**egg**	**1**
1 1/2 cups	**buttermilk**	**375 mL**

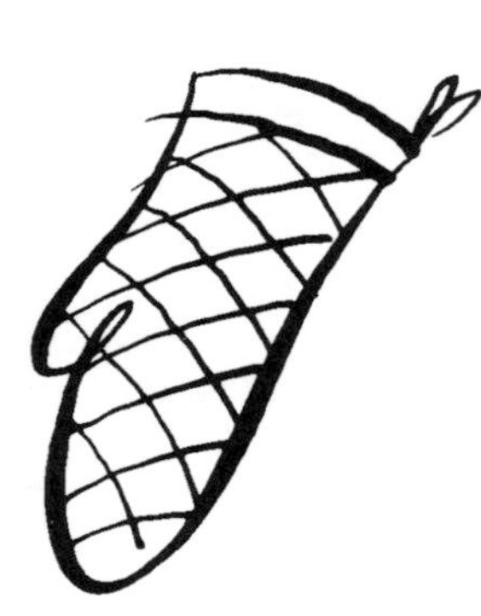

1 Preheat oven to 375°F (190°C).

2 In large bowl, mix together flours, sugar, baking powder, baking soda and salt.

3 Cut in butter until mixture looks like fine crumbs.

4 In another bowl, beat egg and add buttermilk. Add all at once to flour mixture, stirring with a fork to make a soft dough.

5 Turn out onto lightly floured surface and knead gently about 10 times.

6 Cut dough in half. Shape into two round loaves. Place on greased baking sheet. Flatten loaves slightly, and with a sharp knife cut a shallow X-shaped slash on top of each.

7 Bake for 45 minutes or until tester inserted in centre comes out clean and loaves sound hollow when tapped on bottom. Let cool on rack.

PANCAKES

Whether you call them pancakes, hotcakes, griddle-cakes or flapjacks, they're great for a weekend breakfast or brunch. With basic ingredients on hand, whipping up a batch from scratch is as easy as a mix.

1 cup	**all-purpose flour**	**250 mL**
1 tbsp	**granulated sugar**	**15 mL**
2 tsp	**baking powder**	**10 mL**
1/4 tsp	**salt**	**1 mL**
1	**egg**	**1**
1 cup	**milk**	**250 mL**
2 tbsp	**vegetable oil**	**25 mL**

1 In large bowl, mix together flour, sugar, baking powder and salt.

2 In small bowl, beat egg with milk and oil. (Use egg beater or whisk.)

3 Add liquid to dry ingredients. Stir just until almost smooth (there will be a few small lumps).

4 Place large frying pan (preferably non-stick) over medium-high heat on stove for a few minutes. Brush pan lightly with vegetable oil.

5 Using a 1/4 cup (50 mL) measure for easy pouring, pour batter onto pan, making 3 or 4 pancakes with a little space between each.

6 Cook until pancakes are bubbly all over the surface and browned underneath, about 2 minutes. Turn over with a lifter. Cook until browned on the other side, about 1 minute.

7 Cook remaining batter the same way, brushing pan lightly with oil between each batch.

8 Serve hot with butter and maple syrup or other toppings. Makes about 10 pancakes.

Blueberry Topping

In small heavy saucepan, combine **1 cup (250 mL) fresh or frozen unsweetened blueberries, 1/4 cup (50 mL) granulated sugar** and **1 tbsp (15 mL) cornstarch;** mix well. Stir in **1/2 cup (125 mL) water.** Bring to a boil, stirring often; boil gently for 1 minute until sauce is thickened and shiny. Stir in **1 tsp (5 mL) lemon juice.** Makes about 1 cup (250 mL).

Spiced Apple Topping

In small heavy saucepan, combine **2 peeled, thinly sliced apples, 2 tbsp (25 mL) raisins, 2 tbsp (25 mL) granulated sugar, pinch of cinnamon and nutmeg** and **1/4 cup (50 mL) water.** Cook over medium-high heat, stirring often, until apples are tender, about 5 minutes. Serve warm. Makes about 1 cup (250 mL).

FOCACCIA

This savory flatbread is very popular in Italian restaurants and bake shops, but also easy and fun to make at home. Pizza dough can be purchased at many supermarkets and bakeries.

1 lb	**pizza dough (at room temperature)**	**450 g**
1 tbsp	**olive oil**	**15 mL**
1 tsp	**coarse salt *or* ½ tsp (2 mL) regular salt**	**5 mL**
1 tsp	**dried herbs (rosemary, basil, oregano or mixed)**	**5 mL**

1 Preheat oven to 400°F (200°C).

2 Place dough on lightly oiled baking sheet. Flatten dough and press out a rectangle about 12 x 9 inches (30 cm x 23 cm).

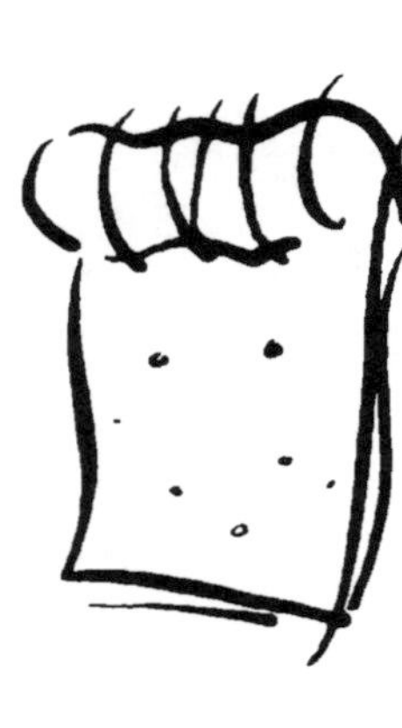

3 Brush with olive oil. With fingers, press indentations into dough to give dimpled surface. Sprinkle with salt and herbs.

4 Bake for about 20 minutes or until golden brown and baked through.

5 Cut into squares or wedges and serve warm. Makes about 8 servings.

VARIATIONS

PARMESAN FOCACCIA: Omit salt. Sprinkle dough with herbs. After 10 minutes of baking sprinkle with ¼ cup (50 mL) grated Parmesan cheese.

ONION & GARLIC FOCACCIA: Omit salt. Sprinkle dough with herbs and sautéed onion and garlic (one small chopped onion, one minced garlic clove cooked lightly in a little olive oil).

HERBED GARLIC BREAD

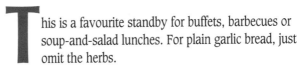

This is a favourite standby for buffets, barbecues or soup-and-salad lunches. For plain garlic bread, just omit the herbs.

1	**loaf crusty Italian or French bread, about 16 x 4 in. (40 cm x 10 cm)**	**1**
½ cup	**butter**	**125 mL**
2	**cloves garlic, minced**	**2**
2 tbsp	**minced chives or green onions**	**25 mL**
2 tbsp	**chopped parsley**	**25 mL**
½ tsp	**dried basil**	**2 mL**
¼ tsp	**dried oregano**	**1 mL**

1 Cut bread into generous ½-inch (1.5 cm) slices.

2 In bowl, combine remaining ingredients. Spread on bread slices.

3 Re-assemble slices into loaf shape. Wrap in foil, leaving top slightly open.

4 Heat in 400°F (200°C) for 15 minutes or until hot. Serves about 10.

VARIATIONS

CRISP GARLIC BREAD: Spread bread slices with herbed or plain garlic butter as above; arrange on baking sheet and heat in 400°F (200°C) oven about 10 minutes.

CHEESE GARLIC BREAD: Add ¼ cup (50 mL) grated Parmesan cheese to butter mixture.

ONE-BOWL WHITE CAKE

This is a good basic cake to make in a hurry. Once you get used to measuring a few ingredients quickly, it's as easy as a mix but has a good buttery flavour and moist texture.

1 ½ cups	**all-purpose flour**	**375 mL**
2 tsp	**baking powder**	**10 mL**
½ tsp	**salt**	**2 mL**
¾ cup	**granulated sugar**	**175 mL**
½ cup	**very soft butter**	**125 mL**
1	**egg**	**1**
¾ cup	**milk**	**175 mL**
1 tsp	**vanilla**	**5 mL**

1 Preheat oven to 350°F (180°C). Grease and flour 8-inch (2 L) square cake pan. (If whole cake is to be removed from pan after baking, line bottom of pan with square of waxed paper.)

2 In mixing bowl, combine flour, baking powder, salt and sugar; stir very thoroughly to mix.

3 Add butter, egg, milk and vanilla. Beat at low speed on electric mixer until moistened, then at medium speed for 1 minute, scraping sides of bowl often.

4 Spread batter evenly in pan.

5 Bake for 35 to 40 minutes or until cake springs back when touched lightly on top, and tester inserted in centre comes out clean.

6 Let cool completely, then spread icing on top *or* turn cake out onto serving plate and ice top and sides. (To turn out, loosen edges with knife and invert cake onto rack; remove pan and then invert cake onto serving plate.)

Easy Strawberry Shortcake

Top squares of white cake with whipped cream and sliced, sweetened strawberries.

VARIATIONS

PINEAPPLE UPSIDE-DOWN CAKE: In bottom of cake pan, spread ¼ cup (50 mL) melted butter and ¾ cup (175 mL) brown sugar. Arrange drained canned pineapple chunks fairly close together on top; add a few pecan halves if desired. Carefully spread cake batter evenly on top. When baked, let cool for a few minutes, then loosen edges of cake with a knife, and carefully invert pan onto large plate.

STREUSEL COFFEECAKE: In small bowl, mix together ¼ cup (50 mL) brown sugar, 2 tbsp (25 mL) flour, ½ tsp (2 mL) cinnamon. Add 1 tbsp (15 mL) melted butter; stir thoroughly with a fork. Sprinkle topping over cake batter in pan before baking. Best served warm.

> **Birthday Cake**
>
> For a big birthday cake place two square cakes side by side on a serving tray to make a rectangle.

CAKE FROSTINGS

VANILLA BUTTER ICING

In bowl, combine **2 tbsp (25 mL) soft butter, 1 cup (250 mL) icing sugar, 2 tbsp (25 mL) milk or cream** and **½ tsp (2 mL) vanilla**. Beat until smooth. If too thin, add a little more icing sugar; if too thick, add a little more milk. Makes enough for top of square cake; to ice top and sides, double the recipe.

VARIATIONS

ORANGE OR LEMON BUTTER ICING: Add 1 tbsp (15 mL) grated orange or lemon rind.

ALMOND BUTTER ICING: Use almond extract instead of vanilla; sprinkle iced cake with chopped almonds.

CHOCOLATE SOUR CREAM ICING

This is soft, shiny and not too sweet. Melt ½ **cup (125 mL) chocolate chips** (in small bowl in microwave or small heavy saucepan over low heat). Add ¼ **cup (50 mL) sour cream**; stir until smooth. Add ½ **cup (125 mL) icing sugar**; beat until smooth. If necessary, chill for a few minutes until thick enough to spread. Makes enough for top of square cake; to ice top and sides, double the recipe.

BROILED TOPPING

Instead of icing, try this yummy topping: In small heavy saucepan, combine ¼ **cup (50 mL) butter,** ½ **cup (125 mL) brown sugar, 2 tbsp (25 mL) milk** and ¾ **cup (175 mL) dessicated coconut**. Bring to boil, stirring; boil gently for 1 minute. Spread over warm baked cake. Place under broiler until bubbly and golden brown; this only takes a couple of minutes; watch carefully so it doesn't burn.

WACKY CAKE

This easy chocolate cake recipe has been around for generations but it's still fun. (It's a good one to teach little kids to make.) The cake is mixed right in the baking pan; or if you prefer, just mix it in a bowl, then pour into pan.

1 ½ cups	**all-purpose flour**	**375 mL**
1 cup	**granulated sugar**	**250 mL**
3 tbsp	**cocoa**	**50 mL**
1 tsp	**baking powder**	**5 mL**
1 tsp	**baking soda**	**5 mL**
½ tsp	**salt**	**2 mL**
⅓ cup	**vegetable oil**	**75 mL**
1 tbsp	**white vinegar**	**15 mL**
1 tsp	**vanilla**	**5 mL**
1 cup	**warm water**	**250 mL**

1 Preheat oven to 350°F (180°C).

2 In ungreased 8-inch (2 L) square cake pan, combine flour, sugar, cocoa, baking powder, baking soda and salt; mix thoroughly.

3 Level off and make 3 holes in mixture; pour oil into one, vinegar into second and vanilla into third. Pour warm water over all; mix thoroughly with fork.

4 Bake for 30 minutes or until tester inserted in centre comes out clean.

VARIATION

CHOCOLATE SNACKING CAKE: In mixing bowl, combine dry ingredients; mix thoroughly. Add remaining ingredients; stir until combined. Stir in ½ cup (125 mL) chopped walnuts. Pour into greased 9-inch (2.5 L) pan and bake.

Easy Chocolate Icing

Top the hot baked cake with **1 cup (250 mL) chocolate chips or a single layer of peppermint patties;** spread when softened.

CARROT CAKE

Moist and spicy carrot cake with cream cheese frosting is an all-time favourite. Most carrot cake recipes make huge cakes; this one is smaller and easier.

1 cup	**all-purpose flour**	**250 mL**
1 tsp	**baking powder**	**5 mL**
½ tsp	**baking soda**	**2 mL**
½ tsp	**salt**	**1 mL**
1 tsp	**cinnamon**	**5 mL**
½ tsp	**nutmeg**	**2 mL**
¼ tsp	**allspice**	**1 mL**
2	**eggs**	**2**
½ cup	**granulated sugar**	**125 mL**
½ cup	**packed brown sugar**	**125 mL**
½ cup	**vegetable oil**	**125 mL**
1½ cups	**grated carrots** (see note)	**375 mL**
½ cup	**raisins (optional)**	**125 mL**

1 Preheat oven to 350°F (180°C). Grease and flour 8-inch (2 L) square cake pan.

2 In small bowl, combine flour, baking powder, baking soda and spices; mix thoroughly.

3 In large bowl, beat eggs. Add sugars and oil; beat well with electric mixer until smooth and creamy.

4 Stir in flour mixture, carrots and raisins; mix thoroughly.

5 Pour into pan. Bake for 40 minutes or until tester inserted in centre comes out clean.

6 Let cool. Frost with Cream Cheese Frosting.

NOTE: Carrots should be finely grated; use a food processor if you have one. Or if your regular grater produces coarse shreds, pile the shredded carrots on a cutting board and chop finely with a large sharp knife. Then measure 1½ cups (375 mL).

Cream Cheese Frosting

With electric mixer, beat together **2 oz (50 g) cream cheese, 2 tbsp (25 mL) but ter** and **1 tsp (5 mL) vanilla.** Gradually beat in enough icing sugar (about 1 cup/ 250 mL) to give smooth spreadable consistency.

APPLE CRUMBLE PIE

Impress your friends with a delicious pie you made yourself; they'll never know how easy it was. For the pastry, you can use a mix or packaged frozen pie shell.

1	**unbaked pie shell (9 inch/23 cm)**	**1**
4	**apples**	**4**
½ cup	**granulated sugar**	**125 mL**
½ tsp	**cinnamon**	**2 mL**
1 tbsp	**lemon juice**	**15 mL**
Topping:		
½ cup	**all-purpose flour**	**125 mL**
¼ cup	**packed brown sugar**	**50 mL**
¼ tsp	**cinnamon**	**1 mL**
¼ cup	**butter**	**50 mL**

1 Preheat oven to 400°F (200°C).

2 Peel and core apples; cut in slices.

3 In bowl, combine apples, sugar, cinnamon and lemon juice. Turn mixture into pie shell, arranging slices fairly evenly.

4 TOPPING: In small bowl, mix together flour, brown sugar and cinnamon; cut in butter until mixture looks like crumbs. Sprinkle over apples.

5 Bake for 40 to 45 minutes or until pastry is golden brown and apples are tender. Let cool until just warm; serve with vanilla ice cream. Makes about 6 servings.

FRUIT CRISP

You can use apples, peaches, pears or a mixture of frui
for this delectable baked pudding.

4 cups	**peeled sliced fruit**	**1 L**
½ cup	**rolled oats**	**125 mL**
¼ cup	**all-purpose flour**	**50 mL**
½ cup	**packed brown sugar**	**125 mL**
¼ tsp	**cinnamon**	**1 mL**
¼ cup	**butter**	**50 mL**

1 Preheat oven to 350°F (180°C).

2 Place fruit in 8-cup (2 L) baking dish.

3 In bowl, combine oats, flour, sugar and cinnamon. Cut in butter until crumbly. Sprinkle over fruit.

4 Bake for 40 minutes or until fruit is tender. Makes 4 servings.

BAKED APPLES

For each serving, use one large apple. Remove the core with an apple corer or small knife. Peel the top one-third of each apple. Place apples in baking dish just large enough to hold them. Fill each core hole almost to top with raisins, then a spoonful of brown sugar, pinch of cinnamon and dot of butter. Pour apple juice or maple syrup (diluted with an equal amount of water), about ¼-inch (.5 cm) deep, around apples. Bake in 350°F (180°C) oven for about 45 minutes or until tender; baste with the juice once or twice during baking. Serve warm, with ice cream or whipped cream.

EASY RICE PUDDING

This is a great way to use up leftover cooked rice and have a delicious dessert, too.

1 cup	**cooked or leftover rice** (see note)	**250 mL**
1 cup	**milk**	**250 mL**
2 tbsp	**granulated sugar**	**25 mL**
¼ cup	**raisins**	**50 mL**
1 tsp	**vanilla**	**5 mL**
1	**egg**	**1**
	Cinnamon or nutmeg	

1 In saucepan, combine rice, milk, sugar, raisins and vanilla. Cook over medium heat until very hot but not boiling, stirring occasionally.

2 In small bowl, beat egg; stir in a little of the hot mixture, then return it to the saucepan, stirring quickly to mix. Keep stirring slowly for about 2 minutes until it thickens slightly (don't let it boil or it will curdle).

3 Remove from heat, cover and let stand until just warm, stirring occasionally. Pudding will thicken more as it cools. Serve warm or chilled. Sprinkle each serving lightly with cinnamon or nutmeg. Makes about 2 servings.

NOTE: The leftover rice should be moist and soft, if it's dry cover with boiling water and let stand until soft, then drain.

CHOCOLATE MOUSSE

This is an impressive dessert for a dinner party, but easy to make with a blender.

1 cup	**chocolate chips (175 g package)**	**250 mL**
⅓ cup	**boiling hot coffee**	**75 mL**
4	**egg yolks**	**4**
4	**egg whites**	**4**
¼ cup	**granulated sugar**	**50 mL**
Garnish:	**whipped cream, grated chocolate**	

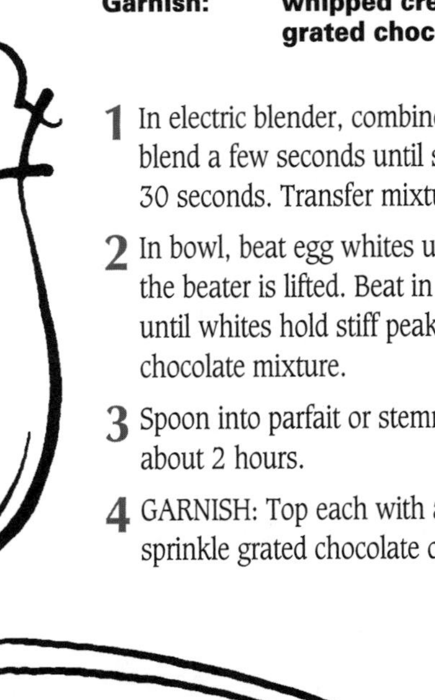

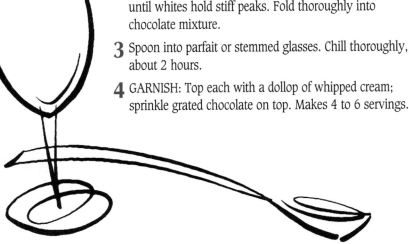

1 In electric blender, combine chocolate chips and coffee; blend a few seconds until smooth. Add egg yolks; blend 30 seconds. Transfer mixture to large bowl.

2 In bowl, beat egg whites until they hold soft peaks when the beater is lifted. Beat in sugar, a little at a time, beating until whites hold stiff peaks. Fold thoroughly into chocolate mixture.

3 Spoon into parfait or stemmed glasses. Chill thoroughly, about 2 hours.

4 GARNISH: Top each with a dollop of whipped cream; sprinkle grated chocolate on top. Makes 4 to 6 servings.

OATMEAL RAISIN COOKIES

Crisp, chewy oatmeal cookies are good for dessert, snacks and brownbag lunches.

¾ cup	**butter or shortening**	**175 mL**
1 cup	**packed brown sugar**	**250 mL**
1	**egg**	
1 tsp	**vanilla**	**5 mL**
1 cup	**all-purpose flour**	**250 mL**
½ tsp	**baking soda**	**2 mL**
½ tsp	**salt**	**2 mL**
1 ½ cups	**rolled oats (quick, not instant)**	**375 mL**
¾ cup	**raisins**	**175 mL**

1 Preheat oven to 375°F (190°F). Grease 2 baking sheets.

2 In large bowl, cream together butter and sugar. Beat in egg and vanilla.

3 In small bowl, combine flour, baking soda, salt and oats; mix thoroughly. Stir into creamed mixture. Stir in raisins.

4 Drop dough by spoonfuls, about 2 inches (5 cm) apart, on baking sheets. Flatten to ½ inch (1 cm) with fork.

5 Bake for 10 to 12 minutes or until golden brown (don't overbake).

6 Let cool on pans about 5 minutes, then remove to wire racks to cool. Makes about 24 cookies.

VARIATION

CHOCOLATE CHIP OATMEAL COOKIES: Omit raisins. Add 1 cup (250 mL) chocolate chips.

Cookie Baking Tips

In most ovens, cookies bake best (without browning too much on the bottom) if the baking sheet is placed just above the centre of the oven. For best results, bake only one sheet at a time. Also, since cookies will continue to bake on the hot sheet for a few minutes after removal from the oven, it's better to slightly underbake than overbake.

NANAIMO BARS

Nanaimo Bars have been made in Canadian homes for decades and are now a popular treat in cafés and bakeshops.

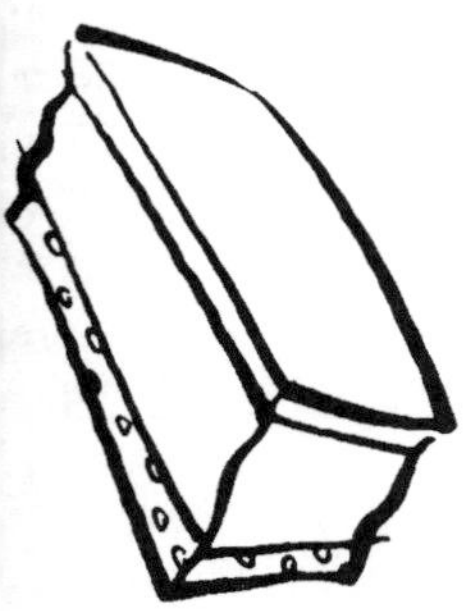

Bottom layer:

½ cup	**butter**	**125 mL**
¼ cup	**granulated sugar**	**50 mL**
⅓ cup	**cocoa (dry unsweetened)**	**75 mL**
1	**egg, beaten**	**1**
1 ½ cups	**graham wafer crumbs**	**375 mL**
1 cup	**flaked coconut**	**250 mL**
½ cup	**finely chopped walnuts**	**125 mL**

Middle layer:

¼ cup	**butter**	**50 mL**
3 tbsp	**milk**	**50 mL**
2 tbsp	**custard powder**	**25 mL**
2 cups	**sifted icing sugar**	**500 mL**

Top layer:

4 oz	**semisweet chocolate**	**125 g**
2 tbsp	**butter**	**25 mL**

1 BOTTOM LAYER: In small heavy saucepan over low heat, melt butter with sugar and cocoa. Add egg and cook, stirring, until slightly thickened, about 2 minutes. Stir in crumbs, coconut and nuts. Press into 9-inch (2.5 L) square cake pan. Chill about 5 minutes.

2 MIDDLE LAYER: Beat together butter, milk, custard powder and icing sugar until very smooth. Spread over bottom layer. Chill until firm.

3 TOP LAYER: In small heavy saucepan over low heat, melt chocolate with butter. Cool slightly and pour over middle layer; jiggle pan to smooth out the chocolate evenly.

4 Chill until chocolate is set but not quite firm. Mark into bars with knife (this prevents cracking if cut when chocolate is cold). Chill until firm. Cut into small bars or squares.

BUTTER TART SQUARES

For a taste of butter tarts without all the trouble of makin them, these gooey bars are the answer.

Base:		
½ cup	**butter**	**125 m**
¼ cup	**granulated sugar**	**50 m**
1 cup	**all-purpose flour**	**250 m**
Topping:		
2	**eggs**	
1 cup	**packed brown sugar**	**250 ml**
2 tbsp	**melted butter**	**25 m**
2 tbsp	**all-purpose flour**	**25 ml**
½ tsp	**baking powder**	**2 ml**
1 tsp	**vanilla**	**5 ml**
1 cup	**raisins**	**250 ml**

1 Preheat oven to 350°F (180°C).

2 BASE: Cream butter with sugar; blend in flour until crumbly. Press into bottom of 8-inch (2 L) square cake pan. Bake for 15 minutes or until lightly browned.

3 TOPPING: In mixing bowl, beat eggs; beat in sugar. Stir i butter, flour, baking powder, vanilla and raisins. Pour over base.

4 Bake for 30 minutes or until set. Let cool and cut in smal squares.

Lemon Squares

Base: Same as for Butter Tart Squares. *Topping:* Beat **2 eggs** with **1 cup (250 mL) granulated sugar.** Stir in **2 tbsp (25 mL) all-purpose flour, ½ tsp (2 mL) baking powder, ¼ tsp (1 mL) salt, grated rind of 1 lemon,** and **3 tbsp (50 mL) lemon juice.** Bake for 25 minutes or until surface is golden brown and centre is almost firm to touch. Cool and dust with icing sugar.

PEANUT BUTTER CEREAL SQUARES

You can make these crunchy unbaked squares in just a few minutes. As a variation, shape the same mixture into small balls. They're almost like candy but do have the redeeming qualities of wholesome ingredients like cereal, peanut butter, nuts, seeds and coconut.

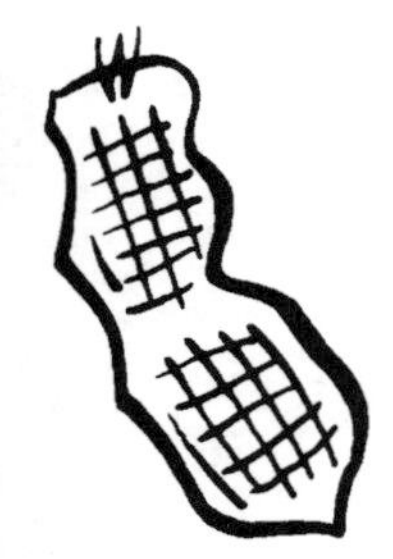

1½ cups	**corn flakes**	**375 mL**
1½ cups	**crisp rice cereal**	**375 mL**
½ cup	**chopped peanuts**	**125 mL**
¾ cup	**corn syrup**	**175 mL**
¼ cup	**packed brown sugar**	**50 mL**
½ cup	**peanut butter**	**125 mL**

Topping:

1 cup	**chocolate chips**	**250 mL**
½ cup	**peanut butter**	**125 mL**

Peanut Butter Cereal Balls

With greased hands, shape the warm mixture into small balls. Place on buttered waxed paper. As they set, press them again firmly into balls. While still sticky, roll in coconut or sesame seeds. Makes about 25.

1. In large bowl, combine cereals and nuts.
2. In small saucepan, heat syrup with sugar just until bubbling, stirring to dissolve sugar.
3. Remove from heat and add peanut butter; stir until smooth. Pour over cereal and mix well.
4. With greased hands, press firmly into buttered 8-inch (2 L) square pan.
5. TOPPING: In small saucepan over low heat, melt chocolate chips with peanut butter, stirring until smooth. Spread over mixture in pan. Chill until firm. Cut in small squares.

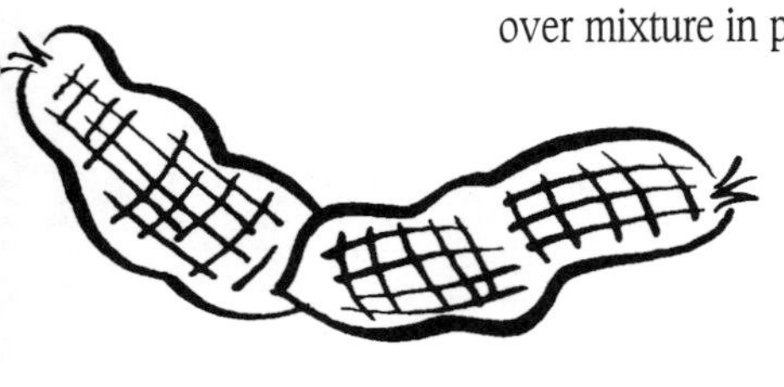

EASY FRUIT DESSERTS

STRAWBERRY DIPPING DESSERT

One of the most delicious ways to eat strawberries is also on of the simplest. Just dip **whole strawberries** first into **sour cream**, then into **brown sugar**. For a buffet, set out pretty bowls of strawberries, sour cream and brown sugar; at a dinner table, provide each person with a plate of strawberrie and small dishes of sour cream and brown sugar.

FRUIT AND CHEESE DESSERT PLATE

This looks very classy but is easy to do. For each guest, arrange a dessert plate with pretty groupings of fruit: **2 or 3 perfect strawberries or a fresh fig**, a **few small slices of melon**, a **tiny bunch of grapes**. Add **2 small wedges of Brie or Camembert cheese**. Place a **sprig of fresh mint** beside the fruit and a **small cookie or sweet cracker** besid the cheese.

PEACHES AND BLUEBERRIES WITH CREAMY ORANGE SAUCE

No one will guess this delicious sauce is so easy. Just spoon over **sliced peaches and blueberries** (or any fruit in season) in stemmed glasses.

CREAMY ORANGE SAUCE: For 4 servings, mix together ½ **cup (125 mL) each of plain yogurt and light sour cream** and ¼ **cup (50 mL) each of granulated sugar and frozen orange juice concentrate** (thawed but undiluted).

EASY ICE CREAM TOPPINGS

MICROWAVE BUTTERSCOTCH SAUCE

In 4-cup (1 L) glass measure or bowl, combine **½ cup (125 mL) brown sugar, ¼ cup (50 mL) whipping cream, 2 tbsp (25 mL) corn syrup and 2 tbsp (25 mL) soft butter**. Microwave on High for 2 minutes; stir. Microwave 1 minute longer; stir until smooth. Stir in **½ tsp (2 mL) vanilla**. Let cool about 10 minutes, stirring occasionally. Pour into small covered jar (sauce will thicken as it cools). Store at room temperature, not in fridge. Makes about ⅔ cup (150 mL).

MICROWAVE CHOCOLATE SAUCE

In 2-cup (500 mL) glass measure or bowl, combine **½ cup (125 mL) chocolate chips, ¼ cup (50 mL) whipping cream, 2 tbsp (25 mL) corn syrup and 1 tbsp (15 mL) soft butter**. Microwave on High 1 minute; stir. Microwave 1 minute longer; stir until smooth. Stir in **½ tsp (2 mL) vanilla**. Let cool about 10 minutes; pour into small covered jar (sauce will thicken as it cools). Store at room temperature, not in fridge. Makes about ⅔ cup (150 mL).

HOT BANANA TOPPING

Sensational on vanilla ice cream. Peel and slice **1 firm banana**. In skillet over medium heat, melt **1 tbsp (15 mL) butter**. Stir in **2 tbsp (25 mL) each of brown sugar and orange juice and a pinch of cinnamon and nutmeg**. Add bananas; cook, stirring gently just until bananas are slightly softened, about 1 minute. Makes 2 servings.

MENUS

You can create easy menus for all occasions using the reci
in this book. Here are some suggestions:

Coffee with Friends

For special people, something fresh from the oven.

Quick Cinnamon Rolls p. 81
or Banana Muffins p. 80
or Streusel Coffeecake p.87

Weekend Brunch

A leisurely treat for two, four or more.

Easy Eggs Benedict p. 49
Fruit Salad Bowl p. 40
Lemon Squares p. 98

Take a Break

Quick munchies when you're with friends.

Grilled cheese sandwiches
or Nachos p. 14
or Veggies with dip p. 13
or Trail Mix p. 21

Pack a Lunch

Mix and match for brown-bagging variety and good nutrition.

Chicken Salad in pita p. 22
or Salmon salad in a croissant p. 22
or Egg salad on pumpernickel p. 22

Oatmeal Raisin Cookies p. 96
or Honey Yogurt Bran Muffins p. 79
or Banana Bread p. 80

Marinated Vegetable Salad p. 37
or Vegetable crudités p. 13
or Fresh fruit

Fresh Market Lunch

Shopping for the ingredients is a pleasure at a Saturday-morning farmers' market.

Tomatoes and Mozzarella with Basil p. 39

Pasta Primavera p. 52

Strawberry Dipping Dessert p. 100

Supper in 15 Minutes

Fast-and-easy one-dish meals; just add a salad.

Baked Potatoes with Toppings p. 41
or Stir-Fried Chicken & Vegetables p. 68
or Fast Pasta p. 52
or Fast Fish p. 76

Soup & Sandwich Supper

Make a toasted sandwich while you reheat some of your good homemade soup.

Clam Chowder p. 27
or Quick Borscht p. 28

Toasted Western Sandwich p. 23
or French Toasted Sandwich p. 23

Oven Dinner

Baking main course and dessert together saves time and energy. Add a green salad or cole slaw.

Oven-Barbecued Spareribs p. 65
or Easy Oven Stew p. 61
or Redtop Meatloaf p. 62

Baked Potatoes p. 41

Hot Biscuits p. 81

Baked Apples p. 93

Vegetarian Supper

Good nutrition and great tastes.

Lentil Vegetable Soup p. 25

Frittata p. 50

Green salad with vinaigrette p. 30

Peaches and Blueberries with Creamy Orange sauce p. 100

Supper Italian-Style

A sure-to-please menu of popular favourites.

Bruschetta p. 20
Easy Lasagna p. 56
Caesar Salad p. 32
Fruit & Cheese Dessert Plate p. 100

Bistro Dinner

A special-occasion menu for two or four. Bon appétit!

French Onion Soup p. 26
Broiled Lamb Chops p. 66
Tomatoes Provençale p. 47
Green Beans with Almonds p. 44
Chocolate Mousse p. 95

Pot Luck Dinner

A dinner party is easy and economical when friends bring one course each; the hosts could make the main dish or salad.

Taco Dip p. 11
and/or Veggies with Dips p. 13
Beef Noodle Casserole p. 63
and/or Chicken & Sausage Cacciatore p. 69
Marinated Veggie Salad p. 37
and/or Greek Salad p. 38
Butter Tart Squares p. 98
and/or Wacky Cake p. 89

Holiday Open House

A finger-food buffet that friends can help prepare and eat!

Taco Dip p. 11
Hot Shrimp Dip p. 12
Veggie Platter with Dips p. 13
Crispy Wings with Dips p. 18
Honey Garlic Wings p. 19
Spiced Nuts p. 21
Nanaimo Bars p. 97

Birthday Bash

Party food that's easy and fun. For a crowd, enlist one or two friends to help cook the fajitas.

Guacamole with tortilla chips p. 15
or Taco Dip with tortilla chips p. 11
Chicken Fajitas p. 16-17
Carrot Cake with Cream Cheese Frosting p. 90
or White Cake with Chocolate Sour Cream Icing pp. 86, 88

Traditional Sunday Dinner

Comfort food for special friends or family.

Roast Chicken p. 72-73
Mashed potatoes
Broccoli with Cheese Sauce p. 46
Orange-glazed Carrots p. 45
Apple Crumble Pie p. 91

Loaf & Ladle Party

Celebrate winter with a warm-up supper after skiing, skating, curling or sleigh-riding. The soups, breads and dessert can all be made ahead and reheated.

Country Kitchen Pea Soup p. 24
Chunky Beef Vegetable Soup p. 61
Wholewheat Soda Bread p. 82
Herbed Cheese Garlic Bread p. 85
Fruit Crisp p. 92

Caribbean Barbecue

A sunny, spicy taste of the Islands for a lively crowd.

Jerk Chicken p. 75
Jamaican Rice and Peas p. 60
Make-ahead cole slaw p. 35
Spiced Banana Coconut Bread with sliced fresh pineapple and mangos p. 89
or Ice Cream with Hot Banana Topping p. 101

RECIPE INDEX